THE REVERENT SKEPTIC

THE REVERENT SKEPTIC

A Critical Inquiry into the Religion of Secular Humanism

BY J. WESLEY ROBB

PHILOSOPHICAL LIBRARY
New York

Copyright, 1979, by Philosophical Library, Inc.
15 East 40 Street
New York, N.Y. 10016

All rights reserved

Library of Congress Catalog Card No. 79-83609
SBN 8022-2245-5

Manufactured in the United States of America

dedicated to—
F.B.S.

Table of Contents

Preface

The impact of modern science upon all facets of contemporary life is self-evident and particularly upon religious attitudes and beliefs. Many people live in two worlds: Their everyday professional or vocational world is dominated by rational and scientific approaches to phenomena while their private world of experience, including religion, is closed off from rational and empirical examination. A great many devout people hold to the validity of religious truths, without question, and have little concern about the consonance of these truths with what they think they know empirically about their world. Events which seemingly contradict natural law are believed on faith in the power of an omnipotent God; thus it is claimed there can be no conflict between science and religion because the ways of God are beyond human understanding and the wisdom of man is folly in the eyes of God. This faith is uncritical and for the most part unexamined.

A great many other people, however, have difficulty fitting

a theistic picture of the world into their predominantly scientific and naturalistic world-view and have no felt or conceptual need for the God-hypothesis. The religious question is placed in ideological limbo and the problem of the ultimate meaning of life goes by default; there is no urgency about answering the religious question since it has no professional or practical payoff.

For the most part, these are highly educated people who find the sources for their own fulfillment through social relationships, concern for other persons, appreciation of the arts, a sense of closeness to nature, pursuit of a wide range of intellectual interests and activities, and devotion to their chosen profession. They are interesting, informed and responsible persons, but for one reason or another, have bracketed out of their lives any formal religious expression. At the same time, they have deeply felt commitments to many basic values: personal integrity, social justice and human rights, dignity of all persons, freedom of inquiry and expression, and similar normative ethical values. They have drawn heavily upon the value structure of their Jewish/ Christian cultural heritage, but find no need to ground their ethical commitments in any theological or metaphysical frame of reference. Broadly speaking, their "religion" is a naturalistic ethical humanism. It is to this group as well as to other thoughtful persons—theists and non-theists alike who feel uneasy about their religious posture and who are still open-minded about the religious question—that I have written this small volume.

The concern of this essay is primarily intellectual and conceptual. Secular humanists deeply committed to their fellow man are in the main persons of integrity and lead fulfilling lives. In no sense do I want to imply that theistic believers are morally better people or are necessarily more self-fulfilled—a stance that would be difficult to defend empirically. Rather, the issue I want to discuss is simply this:

Does a naturalistic philosophical position provide an adequate conceptual or philosophical frame of reference for the richness and depth of human experience? In what ways does a theistic world-view illumine aspects of our experience? This is a critical inquiry and not intended to be a polemic.

In my judgment, the discussion of this and similar theoretical questions is the stuff out of which the intellectual life is made. The academic enterprise is predicated upon the assumption that theoretical issues are of vital importance in a clearer understanding of "reality" and that we are not just playing intellectual games for our own amusement. It is becoming increasingly clear that how one perceives himself and his universe of meaning is of critical relevance to the ways in which a person will use knowledge. When we are dealing with the theoretical questions of religion, there is both the subjective and objective side; thus any truth-claim is the result of human interpretation of experience subject to the possibility of error that is an inescapable aspect of our finitude.

When I was a lad growing up in San Diego, California, I used to watch the San Diego Padres, a baseball team of the Pacific Coast League, play in a ballpark enclosed by a board fence. It was during the depression and I had little money, so I would get to the ballpark early and find a knothole in the fence from which I could see as much of the field as possible. I could seldom find a knothole that had a view of the entire field; thus I would be satisfied if I could see the four bases and part of the outfield. When a ball was hit, I would have to extrapolate from what I could see, from the reaction of the crowd and the movement of the players to determine what was happening. As a result, I could infer from these perceptions if it were a home run, left, right or center field hit or whatever. On occasion I would save enough money to buy a grandstand ticket and there sitting behind home plate I could see all of the action—the "beatific vision" indeed!

This simple experience is analogous, I believe, to the problem I am discussing. Some of us believe that we are watching a *real* "ballgame" while others contend that in all probability what we are seeing is a projection of what we want to see or enjoy. In any event, we all see from our own "knothole," and infer from our experience what we think is happening on the "playing field." It is unlikely that any of us will ever sit in the "grandstand," though a few would like to think they do. How these experiences are conceptualized will vary from person to person and from group to group. Everyone will not discover the same clues in his perceptions, but in our common humanity and in our shared experiences we may find hints about the meaning of life and existence. This essay is an attempt to tread the middle path between the existentialist who would have little regard for any attempt to communicate the nature of being across the boundaries of lived-through experiences, and the pure rationalist or theorist who is more interested in the consistency of his system of thought than he is in its existential adequacy.

In addition, we attempt to examine the world view of naturalistic or secular humanism and some of the influential figures who have helped shape this outlook for modern man. I hope it will help the layperson understand more adequately his own religious attitudes and beliefs. Whether or not my presentation of naturalistic theism as a viable option to secular humanism "checks out," or "rings true" to the reader's experience will be determined by that strange admixture of cognitive and affective elements that are a part of the way we see ourselves and our world. Whatever the reader's reaction, the dialogue must go on.

This book is dedicated to a group of my colleagues and their wives at the University of Southern California who have met monthly for the past sixteen years for serious discussion of a book or article. Our dialogues have ranged from David Hume to Teilhard de Chardin. We represent twelve different disciplines and departments with the University—from the fine arts to neurosurgery. We hold disparate world-views but are bound together, in a deep and personal way, by our common professional ties and our search for truth. For many of us, this experience has been one of the most significant intellectual and spiritual relationships of our lives, and to this group I am particularly indebted for the stimulation and growth they have fostered in my own life. I am also grateful to other colleagues and students with whom I have shared many of the thoughts of this volume and whose intellectual and moral integrity provides a sense of *presence* that makes the academic venture worthwhile.

Several of my colleagues have been kind enough to read the manuscript, either in part or in its entirety. I am particularly grateful to Professors Dallas Willard (Philosophy), Gibson Reaves (Astronomy), William H. Perkins (Speech Communication), and John P. Crossley, Jr. (Religion)—all of whom have been most helpful in their suggestions and criticisms. However, they are in no way responsible or to be held accountable for the ideas expressed herein. Mrs. Rui Sadamura has painstakingly typed the manuscript. Dr. Jill Perkins and Mrs. Emily Henning have given very useful editorial assistance—tasks for which I am indeed thankful. I am also indebted to the Theodore Kurze Foundation for underwriting, in part, the publication of this volume.

University of Southern California

Chapter I

What Is Secular Humanism?

Definitions

There are many forms of humanism as there are many expressions of secularism. For example, within our own time, there is the scientific humanism of Julian Huxley and Max Otto; the philosophical humanism of Paul Kurtz and Corliss Lamont; the existential humanism of Albert Camus and Jean Paul Sartre; the self-realization humanism of Erich Fromm and Abraham Maslow; the Marxian humanism of Herbert Marcuse; the experimental humanism of B. F. Skinner; and the mystical humanism of W. T. Stace. All of these forms of humanism have at least two things in common: (1) A concern for human good, both individually and collectively, and (2) A belief that man must resolve his problems alone and that there is no reality, above or beyond or outside of man, that can provide a resource or energizing power that will assist him in facing the exigencies of human life and society. Man and nature are all there is.

Contemporary forms of secularism are more difficult to identify though they are widely expressed in the life styles of most of us. (1) There is a materialistic secularism that places optimum faith in the ability of wealth and possessions to bring us happiness. It is expressed in its most crass forms in advertisements for goods and services that assume that man's basic material and physical needs are fundamental to his happiness. Since wealth and possessions are power, it feeds on the assumption that man is a power-seeking creature and that material prosperity will assure man's highest happiness.

(2) Closely related to materialistic secularism is hedonistic secularism that seeks fulfillment in life through the pursuit of pleasure and the avoidance of pain. This is illustrated by the headline of an advertisement for a new condominium complex with swimming pools, tennis courts and jacuzzi, "Guaranteed Fun!" The present inclination to identify the "right to the pursuit of happiness" with the right to pursue fun is indicative. This is a far cry from what the Founding Fathers had in mind when they advocated the "rights" of man. Within the popular mind, the distinction between quantitative and qualitative hedonism is seldom made, and the difference between the hedonism of Aristippus and Epicurus is scarcely recognized.

(3) Pragmatic secularism equates the workable with the good. The theme, "Don't set your sights too high, but be realistic in your goals," marks this perspective on the values in life to be sought. The name-of-the-game is compromise and realism; all differences are to be negotiated until a satisfactory settlement is reached. "This is the democratic way," it is argued, and any other attempt to resolve differences is predicated on the assumption that there is a right

and wrong way. It leans toward moral relativism and compromise.

(4) Another type of secularism that is most prevalent among intellectuals is what might be called a spiritual secularism, which places its emphasis upon the life of the creative mind. Some have called it the new religion of culture. It stresses the arts, in all of their forms, and places the creative expressions of men and women throughout history as prime examples of the transcendent power of the human mind and spirit to overcome the viscissitudes of daily life. It provides moments of self-transcendence for its adherents through the theatre, the visual arts, a wide variety of literary forms and through music. It glorifies the outreach of the human spirit toward higher and more expressive forms of creativity. It is a source for the nourishment of the human spirit and is often a replacement for the self-transcending experience that traditional forms of religion attempt to provide.

Again, what these forms of secularism have in common is the implicit view that man and nature constitute the whole of reality and that there is no need to attribute the creative aspirations and expressions of man as having a source within the cosmic sphere of things. The source for such creative urges of man is seldom raised—creativity is accepted for what it is and nothing more. Spiritual secularism is not anti-theological or anti-metaphysical; it is merely atheological and ametaphysical. That is to say, the theological or metaphysical questions are not important. What an aesthetic approach to man and nature may imply will be discussed at a later point in this essay.

Summarizing what we have said, secular humanism is an attempt to place life's meaning within a totally human and naturalistic context. This is its view of reality. Of course the ambiguities of the words "natural" and "human" are a

3

problem to be discussed, but in the most straightforward terms, secular humanism stands within the above described framework of meaning.

Most of us are not consistent in our values and move from one type of secularism to another depending upon mood and circumstance. And in popular American culture, many people combine the secular with the humanistic and with the traditionally religious and seldom face the incongruities of a life style and a set of values that combines all three approaches. Therefore, these distinctions are primarily artificial; however, they do help us see the ambiguity of the culture regarding our values and the need for greater clarification and consistency. There is little question that secularism has been a liberating force and that "man coming of age" has led him to a new sense of responsibility for his own life and future, but the concern of this essay focuses on the existential and conceptual adequacy of a secular world-view that is expressed within a secular humanistic philosophy of life and meaning.

In common usage, the word secular refers to affairs of this world in contradistinction to the world of the divine which is believed to be beyond the world of nature and man. The polarity of the profane and the sacred; the secular and the divine; the finite and the infinite; the mortal and the immortal; the material and the spiritual; and the non-religious and the religious indicates the essentially dualistic view of reality that has characterized most of western philosophical and religious thought. In the popular mind, secular connotes the reality that exists within the space-time, visible and physical order of things. The divine represents another order of being represented by church, synagogue, Scripture, liturgy and clergy. The uneasy comments people make when a clergyman is introduced in an informal social situation reflect a common attitude that such persons are set apart from the ordinary life of men: the clergyman's duty is to remind a society, wedded to material values, of the higher values of the spirit.

Unfortunately, a great deal of western theology has fostered this two-world view—the City of God and the City of Man. Of course, it is not that simple if one fully understands the richness of the Western theological tradition. Nonetheless, the lay public, by and large, clings to the dualism of the two realms of the material and the spiritual. Medieval cosmology placed God in Heaven above and the earth at the center of the universe. Dante's classic, *The Divine Comedy,* uses the ancient Ptolemaic cosmology to draw a graphic picture of rewards and punishments that await mankind in the future life. This bifurcated view of the relationship of God to the world remains to the present day and the notion that God, who is essentially Holy and Other, created the world and has shaped the destinies of men and nations is widely held. Though the Protestant Reformers attempted to overcome the radical separation of the sacred and the profane by stressing that labor and work should be seen as a form of worship, when placed in their proper perspective, the idea of the divine as standing over and above the human lingers.

While the context out of which secular humanists speak concerning their own beliefs is more sophisticated than the common understanding of the word secular, secularists strongly react to a dualistic world-view and, particularly, to the supernaturalism of traditional Jewish and Christian theism. Secular humanists tend to identify all forms of theism with supernaturalism—an issue we will deal with directly in the last chapter of this volume. In addition, secular humanists are agreed in their rejection of any institution that would make a claim to its own unique authority based upon some special revelation. Likewise they resist attempts

5

to understand the world from either a theological or meta-physical perspective. In this discussion, when we refer to secular humanistic approaches to man and his world, we mean a naturalistic world-view, that is, a *belief that the processes of nature can be understood adequately through scientific investigation.* In other words, *nature natures* and there is no need to postulate a non-material reality to explain nature and man. It may be unfortunate that the word secular or naturalistic is viewed as excluding any reality beyond that which can be observed within the natural order. This is in contrast to a theistic world-view that includes a belief in a realm of Being that is both *beyond* and *within* the natural order of things. Secular humanism, as non-theistic, finds no source of meaning or purpose outside of man or nature; hence, as Albert Camus sees it, the universe is silent to man's fate and indifferent to the human condition.

The natural sciences, and more recently the social sciences, have attempted to provide a naturalistic explanation of the world of man, both physical and social, through the application of the procedures of observation and analysis. It is out of this frame of reference that secular or naturalistic humanists attempt to understand man and his world.

As representative of what leading humanists of our own time mean by the word secular or natural, the following statements are helpful:

There is no entelechy, no built-in pattern of perfection. Man is his own rule and his own end. (H. J. Blackham)

A philosophy founded on the agreement that 'man is the measure of all things' can have no room for belief in the intervention of non-material postulates. (Miriam Allen deFord)

6

I myself hold that we have increasing knowledge of our world, and that there is no need to postulate a realm beyond it. (Roy Wood Sellars)

Humanism believes that the nature of the universe makes up the totality of existence and is completely self-operating according to natural law, with no need for a God or gods to keep it functioning. (Corliss Lamont) [1]

Humanists accept the fact that God is dead; that we have no way of knowing that this is a meaningful question. (Paul Kurtz) [2]

Likewise, the word *humanism* needs to be defined for purposes of this discussion. Coming from the Latin, *humanus,* humanism places the highest value upon the human person and gives primary importance to man, his potentialities and well-being within the temporal sphere of his existence. Humanists affirm with Protagoras (440 B.C.) that "Man is a measure of all things, of things that are, that they are; and of things that are not, that they are not—With regard to the gods I know not whether they exist or not, or what they are like. Many things prevent our knowing; the subject is obscure and brief is the span of our mortal life." [3]

The Renaissance, in its attempt to recapture the spirit and form of the Periclean age of ancient Greece, placed optimum value upon the development of human knowledge through man's ability to experience and conceptualize his world. Its resistance to authority of all kinds and its stress upon the importance of human liberation and freedom to break the bonds of ignorance and superstition has provided the intellectual temper and spirit of contemporary humanism. Though the Copernican revolution shattered man's self-image as central in God's universe, the Renaissance endeavored to replace man at the center of the historical and cultural universe seeking no cosmology or theology to justify its claim. Thus the cultural and social revolution, with which humanists identify, was born and the exploration of this planet, its physical properties, geography and peoples, as well as the relationship of the earth to the other planets, became a central focus within western civilization and continues to the present day. Recent explorations in outer space reflect this emphasis and the value we place upon the importance of human inquiry and increased knowledge of the universe.

As we shall note in our summary of *Humanist Manifesto II*, humanism also stresses social values involving certain ethical commitments to man and human well-being.

The following statements by humanists of our own time illustrate the centrality of man and his values within the humanistic perspective:

> ... to commit oneself to Humanist values is to put the welfare of human beings first. (Antony Flew)

> ... an emphasis on the power and dignity of man, on the worth of human personality ... an emphasis on the obligation to respect and cultivate that dignity and worth in oneself and in others. (John Herman Randall, Jr.)

> Humanists respect personality. They recognize the freedom and dignity of human beings. (Gora)

> Humanism calls men to awareness of human possibilities and the choices and the responsibilities before the human individual and the human community. (Algernon D. Black) [4]

Secular Humanism as a Way of Life

There is an increasing number of people within the intellectual community who have deep commitments to the pursuit of truth, as they understand it, and to their fellow man; yet feel no need to place these loyalities within a traditionally religious context. By and large they have divorced themselves from the organized church, not only because of its institutional character, but also because its emphasis, for the most part, is from a world-view that is pre-Copernican and pre-scientific. These are cultured, refined and intelligent people who find their meaning in life through a sense of closeness with nature and through selected social relationships, as well as through the creative expressions in art and literature in their many forms. They identify with the spirit of the Renaissance in its emphasis upon freedom of inquiry unfettered by political and religious authority. Their devotion is to freedom of thought and expression; they are, for the most part, sensitive to issues of human justice and human rights. Their "religion" is the Religion of Culture and Man. Though their level and depth of commitment to humanistic values vary, they are concerned about problems of the dehumanization of man within our society and want to build the kind of society in which human values will be paramount. They are interesting people—well informed about a variety of subjects and attentive to matters of the mind and intellect. They identify with a sub-culture of people who share their interests and commitments. They are thoughtful, reflective and, for the most part, critical of the status quo. They reach out for new experiences and interest that will bring increasing meaning and satisfaction to their lives.

Regarding the questions of religion, they are not hostile. They just do not find it relevant to their own lives; yet, many of them are intellectually interested in religion as a social and cultural force, but find no personal need for religious devotion or dedication. Most of them have had nominal religious backgrounds but have had little or no contact with formal religion since their adolescent years when they dropped out of Sunday School because it was "boring" and had little relevance for their lives. As they spin the television or radio dial, by accident, to a religious program, they are reminded of their unpleasant experiences in church and assume that the religion of their childhood has not changed. Their image of religious faith is that of credulity and when they encounter an educated and informed man who still "believes," they are intrigued and curious. But their curiosity seldom leads them into a serious investigation of religion. They find the source for their own spiritual vitality in those personal experiences that give their life meaning and a sense of fulfillment. Often they are highly trained in their field of specialization and have such a stereotyped view of religion that it cannot intellectually compete with what they think they know through their secular learning and scholarship. The fact is, a junior high school understanding of religion is no contest for a Ph.D comprehension of the biological process.

Several years ago an internationally known physicist came to our campus to deliver a lecture on the subject of "Science and Religion." As a courtesy, I was invited to attend. I must confess I felt like an agnostic at a religious meeting; there was an atmosphere of excitement in the room as the scientific community came to hear what words of wisdom their "prophet" would give them about this subject. He presented a refined and sophisticated view of science and a fourth grade portrayal of religion and left the distinct impression that religion could not stand the test of scientific enquiry; therefore, the only intellectually respectable position is agnosticism. His speech was enthusiastically applauded by his "disciples." During the question period I somewhat timorously inquired, "What books have you read within recent months that deal with the subject of the interface between science and religion?" Whereupon he replied, "None!" and then added, "It would indeed be a unique book that could cast any new light on such an old, old subject as religion." The students broke into applause and laughter at his answer. I then commented that I had read four books within the past two months dealing with his topic coming out of such presses as the University of Chicago and Harvard, and suggested that he do his homework in my field before he addressed another university audience on this subject. The room was hushed with silence; I had challenged the scientific community's "authority" from one of the leading scientific centers of the world. The next day the University school paper ran the headline, "Religion Head Challenges Scientist." Fifty years ago the roles would have been reversed and the headline would have probably read, "Scientist Challenges Religionist." I pointed out, in an interview with a reporter from the paper, that his speech to our community, emphasizing the superiority of science over popular religion, would be as though I went to his institution and talked about a religionist's view of science while never acknowledging the Copernican revolution. Later in the week he called me and out of this encounter developed a personal friendship and hours of dialogue. After our discussions, he often reminded me, "You represent a different view of religion than most people." My only reply was, "Your view of the physical world, as a physicist, is quite different from the layman's view of nature. Why is religion usually reduced to the lowest common denominator in discussions of this type while the most advanced view of science is advanced?" In my own view, when theistic faith is equated with uncritical supernaturalism, there is an inevitable conflict between science and religion, because a theistic understanding of man and nature is an *interpretation* of the meaning of God's relationship to the world and is not "fact" in the empirically verifiable sense that science uses the term. Therefore, religion uses symbols that give meaning and specificity to the religious dimension—a theme we shall develop later.

The student revolt of the counter-culture movement of the 1960's was directed toward "scientism" and "rationalism" because they were too narrow. Castenada's books were on the best seller lists of college bookstores for several years and the retreat away from the rational and the empirical was extreme. These students did not flock to courses in religious studies because they required study and academic work; they were seeking "truth" for themselves in their own way. Timothy Leary, Richard Alpert, and spiritual leaders from the East were their mentors. They organized communes and sought "higher states of consciousness" through a variety of means. It was a reaction against the spiritual sterility and rigidity of a type of mentality that makes absolute its own methodology in the pursuit of truth. To that extent the protest was valid. The tragedy was that it placed religious questions outside of the realm of intellectual examination and the movement became guilty of the same attitudes of certain types of positivism that categorize religious claims for knowledge as noncognitive, though on different grounds. Paradoxically, the response of the counter-culture to religious sources of meaning were seen in the same anti-intellectual way as the "rationalist" or "empiricist" viewed religion against which the movement was reacting.

This volume is an attempt to show that the alternative to agnosticism is neither uncritical faith nor avowed atheism and that the religious response to life can be cognitively meaningful and does not have to rest its case on emotion or subjective feeling. By "the religious response," I mean, a sense of a relationship to a Source of Reality that is both transcendent to and immanent within the natural order, an "ultra-natural" [5] realm of Being and Meaning that, in principle, cannot be adequately explained by scientific methods that are essentially reductionistic. The postulation of such a Source of Meaning contributes to an explanation of the perennial persistence of man's attempt to transcend the limitations of space and time as he seeks fuller and richer meaning for his life than the space-time order can provide.

Secular Humanism as a Philosophy

I suppose in the broad sense any "way of life" could be called a philosophy or even a religion, but we are speaking of philosophy in this context as an attempt to develop a coherent understanding of the whole of human experience as reflected in man's relationship to the world. All efforts to build rationally coherent conceptual structures of meaning are predicated upon assumptions; if the meaning of human experience were self-evidently clear to everyone, there would be little difference in how we perceive our world. Obviously, such is not the case, men's philosophies vary and their attempt to make sense out of their experiences differ. Many secular humanists reject the appellation "religious" because they do not want to be identified with creedal statements and dogmative utterances. It is reported that T.V. Smith, in conversation with E. Eustace Haydon, both of the University of Chicago, said, "I give you my head, my heart, and my hand on Humanism as thought, as ideal and program, but for God's sake do not call it religion." It would be interesting to know Haydon's response, but what prompted Smith's statement is clear: he did not want to be identified with a religion because of its pejorative connotation.

Haydon suggests that humanism closes the gap between

the religious and the secular by providing a philosophy of life that "gives meaning to the human venture and makes earnest with man's effort to create the society that will embody his ethical ideals." [6] Whether or not this statement is more "religious" than "philosophical" is a matter of definition, but it does reflect the concern of many secular humanists that they not be identified with religion or its movements.

Nonetheless, if philosophy is viewed as man's attempt to construct a conceptual understanding of human experience in its many ramifications, certainly secular humanism is minimally a philosophy. Secular or naturalistic humanism can stand on its own feet as a view of man and his world and provide an intellectual framework of meaning that is coherent and self-consistent. Such conceptual structures are at the heart of theoretical science and philosophy; without them experience of the phenomenal world would have no cognitive meaning whatever. Theological structures of meaning are an attempt to make sense out of the data of religious experience and the ways in which men have perceived their experience of God and is just as legitimate an intellectual enterprise as science or philosophy.

Secular humanism, as a philosophy, attempts to provide meaning, intelligibility, conceptual clarity and consistency in its beliefs about man and the world. Placing secular humanism within the traditional fields of philosophic inquiry, it includes in its conceptual framework statements about reality (metaphysics), criteria for knowledge (epistemology), concern for the beautiful (aesthetics), the importance of a sense of obligation and the good (ethics), and the principles of rational and coherent thought (logic). As a philosophy, secular humanism scores on all points.

But the question still remains, does secular humanism qualify as a religion and is there a difference between a philosophy and a religion? The groups who sponsor and publish *Religious Humanism* [7] take a thoroughgoing naturalistic or secular world-view as we have defined it; nevertheless they want to be called religious. The Fellowship of Religious Humanists, founded in 1963, and affiliated with the American Humanist Association and the Unitarian Universalist Association, make clear in their statement of beliefs that its main purpose is "to provide a fellowship devoted to the cultivation of humanistic religious living which springs from the insights of inner experience." The statement further declares that it "aims to defend freedom of thought in religion and to further the application of the scientific spirit to the study of the materials of religion." At the same time, it pledges to "support and preserve the pluralism of modern Humanism through an appreciative understanding of emphases in Humanism that are not specifically religious." [8] Even a cursory glance through the publications of the Journal since its inception in 1967 indicates that the "religious" issue is a contentious one. For example, in the first issue of the publication, one writer makes the distinction between man needing God and man needing religion and points out that man may outgrow the necessity for a belief in God as he turns to science for answers that theistic faith once provided, but he still needs a religion that will provide goals and aspirations by which man can live.[9]

It seems to me that a legitimate claim can be made for the distinction between philosophy and religion. For example it is possible to affirm the validity of theoretical structures of meaning without any personal commitment to them; likewise, one can affirm theological beliefs without any feeling for or commitment to a God or gods. There is no logically necessary connection between one's philosophical system of beliefs and one's personal behavior or commitments. History is replete with men and women who have formulated impressive philosophical and theological systems and yet did not incorporate the implications of these views into their daily lives. As I view it, the major difference between philosophy and religion, by definition, involves such a commitment. When an individual's philosophy becomes his way of life and provides a frame of reference to which he responds with his total being, at that point, it becomes his religion. E. S. Brightman states it well,

> Philosophy differs from religion in that religion consists of attitudes of concern, devotion or worship, and conduct, whereas philosophy is a rational understanding. Both have the same object, the ultimate unity of reality and the source of values in the universe. Religion takes practical and emotional attitudes toward that object, while philosophy seeks to define and interpret it.[10]

The common insistence that to be religious involves believing and responding to a belief in a personal God is too narrow and provincial because it would exclude most of the religions of mankind. Only three of the eleven historic religions believe in a monotheistic God, namely, Judaism, Christianity and Islam. Therefore, any effort to define religion must be more inclusive. The attempts to define religion have been wide and varied. A few illustrations will suffice:

> The dream of the human spirit—essentially an earthly dream. (Ludwig Feurbach)

> Whatever introduces genuine perspective. (John Dewey)

> The recognition of all duties as divine commands. (Immanuel Kant)

The state of being grasped by an ultimate concern. (Paul Tillich)

The conservation of the highest values. (E. S. Ames)

The belief in an ever living God, that is, in a Divine Mind and Will ruling the Universe and holding moral relations with mankind. (James Martineau)

Our consciousness of the beyond. (Wm. Ralph Inge)

Religion is the consciousness of our practical relation to an invisible, spiritual order. (Josiah Royce) [11]

These widely disparate descriptions of religion have no common thread and reflect primarily the core of what the individual philosopher holds to be central within a religious perspective. My own definition of religion endeavors to include the major aspects of all of the major historical religions and those relatively new movements that are protagonists of a certain philosophy or way of life, for example ideologies such as Marxism and the forms of Communism that have emerged out of a Marxist understanding of man and history. It seems to me that the three elements that characterize *a religion* are: (1) An attitude involving a person's primary response to an object, be it a god, or the state, or other persons, that is considered of ultimate value, and hence has a priority in life unlike other objects to which one is dedicated. (2) This commitment evokes responses of awe and reverence eliciting certain feelings and emotions that are distinctive and indigenously related to the object of devotion. (3) The commitment, and all that it evokes, affects conduct and places upon the individual a sense of duty that is greater than most other claims upon his life. This ethical sense derived from his commitment and devotion, brings direction and meaning to his life and behavior. In brief, my definition of religion is as follows:

Religion is an attitude toward that which is believed to be Ultimate evoking responses of awe and reverence which in turn affect and set standards for behavior.

By this definition, secular humanism is a religion, as we shall note, in the *statement of faith* enuciated in *Humanist Manifesto II.*

Secular Humanism as a Religion

Humanist Manifesto, appearing in 1933 in *The New Humanist,* VI, 3, written by Roy Wood Sellars affirmed that humanism was a naturalistic philosophy and also a religion because it provided a frame of reference by which men could pursue the good life. Furthermore, he pointed out that humanism involved human aspirations and commitments undergirded by faith and hope. As Edwin H. Wilson points out,[12] ethical humanism grew out of the efforts of the American Ethical Union and moved from Felix Adler's idealism to a more naturalistic posture. In 1952 the movement was internationally organized in Amsterdam and was called The International Humanist and Ethical Union. In some countries humanist groups receive subsidies from the state and are recognized as an alternative faith and consequently have the status of a religion. In 1973 there were thirty-three different humanist associations in twenty-three countries affiliated with The International Humanist and Ethical Union. The basic affirmation that unites all of these groups is their commitment to the good life here on earth and the development of a kind of society where human potentialities for growth and creativity can thrive and flourish. Though many of these groups are not anti-church or

18

anti-religious in the conventional meaning of these terms, they are, by and large, non-theistic and broadly speaking naturalistic in their philosophical position.

Forty years after the appearance of *Humanist Manifesto,* signed by a distinguished group of philosophers, scientists and other citizens, *Humanist Manifesto II* [13] was published bearing the names of an equally outstanding group of scholars and laymen. The second *Manifesto* bore the essential stamp of the first version, but was more explicit in its social principles, and was more realistic about the implications of the Nazi holocaust for a view of man's potentialities for evil and destruction. Also, the new statement was more conscious of the possibilities for human good and evil that modern scientific and technological advances have made available.

Using this second document as a paradigm, does secular humanism qualify as a religion? Does it provide sources for devotion and commitment that give life meaning and direction? Has it explicit ethical views that will provide guidelines and principles for individual and group behavior? What are its beliefs?

(1) *Beliefs about Religion.* It is interesting that the *Manifesto* affirms the human need for "dedication to the highest ethical ideals" and the "cultivation of moral devotion and creative imagination" as "an expression of genuine 'spiritual' experience and aspiration," as legitimate forms of religious expression. But then it adds a disclaimer that in no way do such affirmations involve a belief in a notion of revelation, God, ritual, or creed that would place such beliefs above human needs. It further affirms that the insistence upon the existence of a supernatural being is "either meaningless or irrelevant," to the fulfillment of the needs of man. Though it derives many of its ethical teachings from the great religions of mankind, humanism is not dependent upon them for the affirmations of its moral principles. As

for a teleological world view, secular humanists find "no divine purpose or providence" for humankind. Man is a product of natural evolutionary processes and can be explained adequately through an understanding of biological, social and cultural development. Secular humanists also are suspicious of those who profess to reinterpret traditional religious views in the light of new historical and scientific knowledge because they are often "obscurantist" and perpetuate "old escapisms and dependencies."

(2) *Beliefs about Ethics.* Ethics derives its source from human experience and needs no theological or ideological sanctions to justify its claims. Ethical standards are justified only as they enrich human values; hence all trends toward dehumanization are viewed as evil because they limit man's fulfillment and full realization. Reason is the means through which social problems can be resolved and technological and scientific advances can be directed toward human good. Reason must be "tempered by humility," since no one person or group possesses full knowledge of the right and the good. Critical intelligence, tempered by love and caring, is the path toward a better society and world for mankind. Along with religion and ethics, other cultural forms of human creativity in the arts, literature, and music enhance man's "sense of wonder," as he seeks enlarged areas for self expression.

(3) *Beliefs about the Individual.* Central to the humanist perspective is "the preciousness and dignity of the individual person." All forms of dehumanizing control of man's freedom are rejected whether they be religious, political or social. "Maximum individual autonomy," consistent with "social responsibility," is affirmed. Tolerance of others' behavior is a prerequisite to a free society; this principle applies to the acceptance of a variety of life styles which may neither be conventional nor widely accepted within the society as a whole. The key issue is that human persons be

respected in their own right and not be exploited for the selfish ends of another.

(4) *Beliefs about a Democratic Society.* Here human rights and civil liberties are fundamental including freedom of speech and the press, and those other freedoms central to being a free person within a free society. Humanists would implement and extend the principles of human freedom as stated in the Magna Carta, the Bill of Rights, the Rights of Man, and the Universal Declaration of Human Rights. The purpose of government is to facilitate human liberty and the right of the individual to determine his own destiny; thus participatory and decentralized democracy become the instruments for bringing about these values. The separation of church and state is affirmed and in no way should the state espouse any single ideology or religion. Economic systems should be evaluated in terms of their ability to increase the economic well being of all groups and persons and thus enhance the quality of life for everyone. Discrimination because of "race, religion, sex, age, or national origin," ought to be eliminated; each person should be viewed as having equal moral equality. This includes the disenfranchised within the society—the elderly, retarded, handicapped, imprisoned—"all who are neglected or ignored." Implementation of humanistic values should be the aim of our educational institutions since all have "the right to universal education."

(5) *Beliefs about World Community.* Limits imposed by national sovereignty should be transcended; every effort should be made toward the building of a world community based upon principles of law and order implemented by a world community. In order to move toward this achievement, war must be renounced as a means for settling disputes. Peaceful adjudication of differences must be achieved through international law and international courts. All forms of technological, agricultural, economic and medical

assistance must be provided to those peoples who are in the third and fourth worlds. The wide disparity between wealth and poverty must be resolved throughout the world. If full international cooperation, in all aspects of cultural, scientific and technological life is achieved, the humanist ideal of a more humane world would be possible. The final affirmation of faith and hope appearing in the last sentence of the *Manifesto* is: "We believe that humankind has the potential intelligence, good will, and cooperative skill to implement this commitment in the decades ahead."

Returning to the three elements that characterize a religion, we find that humanism as outlined in *Humanist Manifesto II* is a religious point of view. In the first place, it recognizes the human person to be of essential and intrinsic value worthy of our primary and full commitment, unlike other objects and values to which we are dedicated. In other words, the object of commitment bears within itself a quality of Ultimacy. Secondly, the quality and demand this object of devotion places upon us creates a quality of caring and loving that distinguishes it from other things in our lives. Hence, human persons are revered for what they are and what they might become. For example the humanist would stand in "awe" and "reverence" when a newborn child, however conceived—out of love or carelessness—comes into this life. This affective response is psychologically similar to other great moments in our lives when we have been touched in a uniquely human way. It may be felt in relationship to nature, with another person or persons, or in a new discovery. In a sense we are grasped by a feeling, not unlike what Abraham Maslow calls "peak experiences," that deeply move our inner being. In the third place, humanism, as described earlier, involves a commitment to profoundly significant ethical principles that shape and direct human conduct. In its emphasis upon the unique aspects of every human situation, it calls for humane action that will enhance the personal quality of all relationships within the society and the world as a whole. These three ingredients: an ultimate value; affective responses of caring and love; and principles of moral responsibility and duty provide a religious conceptual framework.

NOTES

1. The preceding statements are from essays by each of the authors appearing in Paul Kurtz, (Ed.), *The Humanist Alternative*. (Buffalo: Prometheus Books, 1973). H. J. Blackham, "A Definition of Humanism," p. 36; Miriam Allen deFord, "Heretical Humanism," p. 82; Roy Wood Sellars, "The Humanist Outlook," p. 136; Corliss Lamont, "Naturalistic Humanism," p. 129. Used by permission.

2. Paul Kurtz, (Ed.), *Moral Problems in Contemporary Society*. (Englewood Cliffs: Prentice Hall, Inc., 1969). Essay by Paul Kurtz, "What Is Humanism?" p. 4.

3. From Charles M. Bakewell, *Source Book in Ancient Philosophy*. (N.Y.: Charles Scribner's Sons, 1907), p. 67.

4. Statements are from Paul Kurtz, (Ed.) *The Humanist Alternative, op. cit.,* Antony Flew, "Scientific Humanism," p. 112; J. H. Randall Jr., "What Is the Temper of Humanism?" p. 58; Gora, "Humanism and Atheism," p. 147; Algernon D. Black, "Our Quest for Faith: Is Humanism Enough?", pp. 74, 75. Used by permission.

5. A term used by Paul Weiss to denote another dimension of meaning man experiences. He uses this term to avoid the problems of a supernaturalism that would

suggest God's intervention in the natural order. See *The God We Seek,* (Carbondale: So. Illinois Univ. Press, 1964).

6. A. Eustace Haydon, "Is Scientific Humanism Religious?" *Religious Humanism,* Volume II, Number 2, Spring, 1968, p. 50.

7. *Religious Humanism* is published by The Fellowship of Religious Humanists and affiliated with The American Ethical Union, The American Humanist Association, and The Unitarian Universalist Association.

8. *Religious Humanism,* Vol. I, Number 1, Winter, 1967, p. 64.

9. W. S. Fisk, " 'God is Dead'—Long Live Religion!" *Religious Humanism,* Vol. I, Number I, Winter, 1967, pp. 11-14.

10. Edgar S. Brightman, *A Philosophy of Religion.* (N.Y.: Prentice-Hall, Inc. 1940), p. 22.

11. I am indebted to two sources for these definitions of religion: James H. Leuba, *A Psychological Study of Religion.* (N.Y.: The Macmillan Co., 1912); John B. Magee, *Religion and Modern Man.* (N.Y.: Harper and Row, 1967).

12. Kurtz, *op. cit., The Humanist Alternative.* Essay by Edwin Wilson, "Humanism's Many Dimensions," pp. 15-19.

13. *Humanist Manifesto II* is published by the American Humanist Association, Humanist House, 125 El Camino del Mar, San Francisco, Calif. 94121. The substance and references in this section of the chapter are taken from this document.

Chapter II

The Modern Philosophical Roots of Secularism

The Period of Transition

Prior to the modern period, Platonic metaphysics profoundly influenced medieval thought in its emphasis upon the separation of the world of ideas and forms from the space-time world of physical nature. The realm of universals was seen as real while the world of particulars was perceived as an appearance only. The famous Allegory of the Cave in Book VII of *The Republic* illustrates Plato's view that most men are enslaved by the world of sense. It is only through the discipline of the mind that man can free himself from the appeal of the physical world and comprehend the realm of universals and forms, and beyond that, the noetic vision of Truth, Beauty and Goodness. In the third century A.D., Platonism was revived in the thought of Ammonius Saccas and widely disseminated by

25

his pupil, Plotinus, in the philosophy of Neo-Platonism. Plotinus held that the Absolute or God existed above and beyond all finite reality and emanating from Him were the World-Mind (Ideas and Forms), the World-Soul (Individual Souls) and Matter (Physical World). In the final analysis, matter was viewed as nonbeing. Reality consisted of eternal principles that find expression through the realm of ideas and forms. This system was an attempt to overcome the radical dualism of Platonic thought—the separation of the world of the mind from the world of the senses. The influence of Neo-Platonism upon Augustine's thought is well known, and though Augustine never resolved the monistic-dualistic issue in his metaphysics, his theological and philosophical view did influence the Middle Ages for almost a thousand years. One of the reasons Aquinas found Aristotle's philosophy so appealing was the Aristotelian attempt to identify form as existing *within* matter in contrast to the separation of form *from* matter as in Platonic thought.

The reason I have given this brief historical statement is to show that in both the dualism of Plato and the attempted monism of Plotinus, matter is seen as metaphysically unreal—Being exists beyond and above the physical world. Aristotle attempted to bring the physical world back into metaphysical focus by accepting it as real. He believed that each thing within nature bore within itself its own form or essence that could not be reduced to any physical properties. This gave meaning and identity to each perceived object as it exists in relationship to a class or species of which it is a part. Thus the spiritual and the physical were combined and the essential nature of each existent thing was preserved. It was widely believed throughout the Middle Ages that physical reality could not be understood adequately apart from assuming that, in some way, the material world existed in an intimate and organic relationship to the divine. This organic relationship was questioned and the space-time world was seen as existing independently from any theological or metaphysical realm of being; the seed for the secularism of later periods was planted. Viewing the natural world as devoid of any spiritual elements took time to develop, but as man began to understand the world of which he was a part through the methods of observation and structured investigation, the notion that there were non-material forces at work within the processes of nature began to recede into the background and were seen as rooted in superstition and ignorance. If a theological understanding of nature were to be held at all, its claims had little or no bearing upon scientific methods of investigation and discovery. As I have suggested, the development of a completely naturalistic world view did not happen all at once, but there were two important figures that were precursors of such a view: Roger Bacon (c. 1220-c. 1292) and Francis Bacon (1561-1625), both English men of letters and science who played a significant role in the transition from medieval to modern thought.

Although we have only fragments of Roger Bacon's writings, it is clear from our limited knowledge that his primary goal was to understand the secrets of nature through observation and experimentation. In fact, he was one of the first thinkers to use the term, "experimental science," a word that is common in our vocabulary today. He has been called the father of the experimental method and provided a great deal of the spirit and temper of scientific investigation that followed. In addition, he saw the relationship of mathematics to a study of nature—a notion associated with Pythagoras that became again central in scientific work two centuries later. He was most critical of the investigations that preceded him, notably Aristotle's, and insisted that all claims for knowledge of the physical world should be checked by further examination and experimentation. His emphasis was upon the dignity of the natural man and his ability to discover the facts about the physical world through the powers of reason and observation. He believed that the key to unlocking the mysteries of nature was through inquiry and experimentation. At the same time, he was a part of his time. He saw both science and philosophy as handmaidens to theology, in that true science would not contradict true theology. However, his belief that it was the right of man to investigate freely the nature of the physical order jeopardized his relationship with the Church and finally led to his fourteen years of imprisonment. His acceptance of the division of the natural from the supernatural reflected the medieval thought of his day and the beliefs of the Franciscan Order of which he was a member. In spite of all of this, his contributions as an inventor and experimental investigator made him a key figure in the movement away from the dogmas of his own day that were not grounded in observable data, but were speculative notions that were authoritatively taught as true. He provided the intellectual initiative and courage that influenced the inquisitive minds of men who followed him in the period of the Renaissance.

Francis Bacon appeared three hundred years later as a second important transition figure. His interests and influence ranged from politics to science, but his major contribution to his and our own time was his view that the primary purpose of knowledge was to give man greater mastery over nature and to free man from the prejudices and superstitions that limit his full understanding. He was a very practical philosopher. He was not interested in the ultimate nature of things; he believed they had little bearing upon the fortunes of men. At the same time, he believed that man belonged to three Kingdoms: (1) The Kingdom of God where by Divine Grace he is forgiven of his sins; (2) The Political Kingdom where law and justice prevail, given by God to ruling powers; and (3) The Kingdom of Nature over which man at creation was given domination. The source for the first two Kingdoms is the revelation given by God in the Bible while the natural world is to be understood by man as it is structured by physical and natural causes. It is this latter realm toward which Bacon directed his interests.

He was attracted to Democritus and the Greek atomists who gave a materialistic interpretation of the structure of physical reality. Though Bacon was interested in the *forms* of nature, this was quite different from Aristotle's view of *essences* as existing within particular objects; Bacon held that forms are the latent processes and structures in nature that can be understood through the analysis of phenomena into simpler structures. The method by which such structures could be understood was through induction as the observer moves from facts to laws arrived at through the inductive process. The inductive leap must be pursued cautiously, he warned. For example, when investigating a phenomenon, special attention must be given to the exception to the rule, or what he calls the "negative instance." If we believe that some particular cause brings about a certain type of illness but discover that the suspected cause is not present in all cases, we must reconsider our hypothesis and search for other possible causes. We must move step by step from particulars to our inferences regarding them. We must validate our inferential judgments by continual observation and experimentation. He states his view succinctly in Book One of *The New Organon* when he says, "Man, being the servant and interpreter of Nature, can do and understand so much and so much only as he has observed in fact or in thought of the course of nature. Beyond this he neither knows anything nor can do anything." [1] He believed that the false ways of looking at things, what he calls Idols, are due to the weaknesses of our anthropocentric tendencies. These are worth stating because they are insightful and indicate his commitment to the discovery of "objective truth."

First of all, he states that there are only two ways of discovering and searching for truth. The one stems from "the senses and particulars to the most general axioms, and from these principles, the truth of which it takes for settled and immovable, proceeds to judgment and to the discovery of middle axioms ... The other derives axioms from the senses and particulars, rising by a gradual and unbroken ascent, so that it arrives at the most general axioms last of all. This is the true way, but as yet untried." [2] His distinction between the Idols of the human mind, on the one hand, and the Ideas of the Divine, on the other hand, is significant; he identified the former with "empty dogmas," and the latter with "the true signatures and marks set upon the works of creation as they are found in nature." [3] This would indicate that he believed that the structures of nature may be interpreted as expressive of the "works of creation," but such a view had little or no bearing upon how these structures were to be discovered or understood in relationship to the axioms and laws that were to be established by the inductive method. What are the Idols that impede our true understanding of nature's ways and beset men's minds? They are: The Idols of the Tribe; Idols of the Cave; Idols of the Market Place; and Idols of the Theater.

(1) Idols of the Tribe. The tribe or race of men are prone to see things according to their own perceptions or "according to the measure of the individual and not according to the measure of the universe." [4] Our human understanding is like a "false mirror," mingling its own nature with the nature of things as they are. A case in point is the tendency of the human understanding to posit more order and uniformity in nature than it finds. Furthermore, the human understanding wants to believe its own opinions regardless of the evidence against such views, as in the case of select-

30

ing the evidence that confirms our notions and neglecting data that do not support our beliefs. Men seem to delight in those vanities of thought in which they seemingly find confirmation in experience, but pay little or no attention to those experiences that do not. The search for final causes in nature is fruitless, though Bacon acknowledges that there is a restlessness in man that seeks some cause prior to nature. Causes, he affirms, can only be stated as they are discovered. This is essentially an empirical problem and not a metaphysical one; Bacon's interests are cast within the limits of empirical investigation leaving the larger metaphysical and theological questions unanswered—such issues are matters of faith and not knowledge.

(2) Idols of the Cave are individual idols distinctly personal in contrast to the errors common to all men. These idols are determined by individual nature and temperament; by education and contact with others; by the heroes the individual may admire and esteem; or by other influences that are a part of his environment. Each person has interests that are uniquely his own; hence, he must be careful not to distort his perception of reality as a whole by his preferences. Bacon felt that Aristotle had made his natural philosophy "a mere bond servant to his logic," thus distorting factual perceptions of the natural world. Bacon gives sound advice for our own time when he suggests that too much reverence for the ancient views or too much emphasis upon modern ideas can lead the inquirer away from the more desirable mean between the two. "Truth," he said, "is to be sought for not in the felicity of any age, which is an unstable thing, but in the light of nature and experience, which is eternal." [5] Also, he believed that we should hold with suspicion any affectation or belief that becomes our favorite subject or interest. Regarding such matters, he admonishes, "keep the understanding even and clear." [6]

(3) The Idols of the Marketplace are those of common commerce and discourse. Here words are used unprecisely and with no clarity of meaning. As the result, the "unfit choice of words" distorts and obstructs the understanding. Bacon cites two forms of the inappropriate use of words: (a) Names given to things that do not exist and to which nothing in reality corresponds and (b) Names of things that exist but are ill defined and hastily derived from realities. Illustrations of the former are such names as Prime Mover, Planetary Orbits, Element of Fire, and the like, that have their source in unproven theories. The other class of words are those referring to aspects of nature that are ambiguous, for example, the word *humid.* It is a variable word that can have a variety of meanings and connotations depending on the context in which the word is used. His call is for greater accuracy of the words used to describe phenomena.

(4) Idols of the Theater refer to those dogmas of philosophy and science that have imbedded themselves upon our consciousness. He looked at these like stage plays, representing the world of our own creation. These include principles and axioms in science which have been uncritically received from the past without further investigation and testing. As he saw it, the problem is that systems of thought have been perpetuated from one generation to another without examining them in the light of new knowledge; in fact, when they are challenged it is usually to the detriment of the challenger who is often persecuted for his ideas. These idols are based on "too narrow a foundation of experiment and natural history." Here he was attacking those philosophies that take only a few common instances or experiences, and without weighing them or examining them, "leaves all the rest to meditation and agitation of wit." [7] In addition, there are the philosophers, he contends, who mix their philosophy with their theology and with other traditions and, as the result, perpetuate groundless

beliefs. Equally dangerous is the empirical philosopher who would base his dogmas upon "the narrowness and darkness of a few experiments." Regarding the relationship of philosophy to theology and what he calls "the unwholesome mixture of things human and divine," he urges that "we be sober-minded, and give to faith that only which is faith's." [8]

For him the true way for the interpretation of nature is through demonstrable experience. He says,

> The true method of experience first lights the candle, and then by means of the candle shows the way; commencing as it does with experience duly ordered and digested ... and from it educing axioms, and from established axioms again new experiments ... a method rightly ordered leads by an unbroken route through the woods of experience to the open ground of axioms.[9]

Summarizing Francis Bacon's importance for our study, he was one of the earliest philosophers to outline clearly the realms legitimate for empirical investigation and the methods by which axioms and laws could be responsibly stated. At the same time, he separated the rational and empirical enterprise from matters of faith and, though he included in his Natural Philosophy speculative problems concerning formal and final causes (metaphysical questions), his primary interest was in efficient and material causes (physics). It was this faith/reason dichotomy that finally led to the dissolution of faith, and left observation and experimentation, and what could be inductively established, to stand as hypothetical structures of meaning that could be subjected to further testing and validation. As was the case in many other transition figures of his time, Bacon did not intend to destroy religious faith; rather, he placed theological discourse in the peripheral realm of the spirit. Thus the roots of a naturalistic world-view began to take form. It would be unfair to call Francis Bacon a "naturalist" in the full meaning of that term, but he did look at nature and its processes in terms of the laws that could be extrapolated from the gathering of data. Also he attributed the structures within nature to the divine intent at the time of creation. Be that as it may, he laid the foundation stone of English empiricism and the scientific method.

Any complete account of the transition from the medieval to the modern view of man and nature would have to include Nicolaus of Cusa, Copernicus, Tycho Brahe, Bruno, Galileo, Kepler, and most importantly Isaac Newton, but it has not been our purpose to present a full historical background for naturalistic philosophy and science. We have seen, however, how the ground was broken leading to a naturalistic world-view as early as the 13th century by Roger Bacon and again in the crucial 16th century by Francis Bacon. Their willingness to challenge the dogmas of their own time, both in theology and philosophy, paved the way for the refreshing spirit of the Renaissance that provided mankind with new hope for the future and the improvement of man's lot in the world.

In addition to all of these, there are four key figures that helped shape the modern mind. The mind-set and worldview of many people within the academic community have been influenced by a number of important men of learning, namely: David Hume of the 18th century, August Comte and Charles Darwin of the 19th century, and Sigmund Freud of the 20th century.

David Hume's Skepticism

David Hume (1711-1776) is a key figure in our study of the transition from the rationalism of Descartes and Leibnitz to the empiricism of later periods. The rationalists held to the notion of *innate ideas,* that is, there are certain self-evident truths that the intellect can know as certain that are neither derived from, nor necessarily confirmed by, experience. The emphasis here is on the priority of conception over perception. The only way to transcend the space-time order is to seek those indubitable truths that are self-evident to every rational mind. Such notions as God and the thinking self are "clear and distinct" and hence are undeniable and certain. It is interesting that our nation's Founding Fathers endeavored to defend the "self-evident" character of the "inalienable rights" of man from the same standpoint—a conviction central to the rationalistic temper of the Enlightenment. In contrast, Locke held to the view that the intellect, at birth, is a *tabula rasa,* a blank tablet, as it were, upon which experience writes its story. He saw no evidence that men either think alike or hold to common ideas. The experiences of the individual determine the ways in which the person thinks and believes. Even if there were innate ideas it would be impossible to determine those which were innate and those which were learned; hence the assertion regarding innate ideas cannot be defended. Because of this ambiguity, logical propositions, predicated upon such rules as the law of non-contradiction, for example, are useful tools for assuring consistency of thought and need not be attributed to the innate structure of the mind. Locke's notions created a revolution of thought and had profoundly significant implications for the conviction that there were certain universal and self-evident moral and religious truths that would appeal to all rational minds.

David Hume, born seven years after Locke's death, carried the empirical message further to the point of a consistent skepticism about all claims for knowledge and thus helped formulate the spirit of skepticism so prevalent in our own time. He was an iconoclast of the first order and was refused professional appointments during his career at both the Universities of Edinburgh and Glasgow because of his beliefs. He shook the established way of thinking to its foundations and aroused philosophy from its "dogmatic slumbers" (a comment made by Kant about the influence of Hume's philosophy upon his thought).

Hume's significance is paramount if we are to understand the scientific mentality and the assumptions upon which it is predicated. Hume challenged two of the fundamental ideas of western philosophical reflection up to his time, namely, the notion of substance and the idea of necessary causality. Both beliefs, he affirms, are relations between ideas and cannot be either proved or substantiated by logic or experience. This shattered the logical and metaphysical assumptions prior to his time and denied the possibility of certainty about any realm of knowledge. In Section I of his *Enquiry* he objects to most metaphysical speculations because of their obscurity and their propensity for uncertainty and error. Such speculations arise, he says, "either from the fruitless efforts of human vanity, which would penetrate into subjects utterly inaccessible to the understanding, or from the craft of popular superstition." [10] And at the end of Section XII he reacts more negatively to theological and metaphysical speculation when he adds, "If we take in our hand any volume of divinity or school of metaphysics, for instance, let us ask, *Does it contain any abstract reasoning concerning quantity or number?* No. *Does it contain any experimental reasoning concerning matter of fact and existence?* No. Commit it then to the flames; for it can contain nothing but sophistry and illusion." [11] The only way to free philosophy and learning from vain speculations, that give it the "air of science and wisdom," is to examine the nature of human understanding. Thus, by showing how and what we can or cannot know and the fruitlessness of inquiries about realms of Being posited by metaphysicians and theologians, we can demonstrate their falsity and meaninglessness.

Hume lays his claim upon the view that all ideas are derived from experience. His epistemological analysis involves the distinction between impressions and thoughts. Impressions are perceptions including those of sense as well as love, hate, desire and will. These are forceful, vivacious and immediate. Thoughts or ideas are less "forceful impressions" and include such activities as memory and imagination. The so-called creative power of the mind, he says, "amounts to no more than the faculty of compounding, transposing, augmenting, or diminishing the materials afforded us by the senses and experience . . . all our ideas or more feeble perceptions are copies of our impressions or more lively ones." [12] In other words, the intellect has no capacity for generating thought in and of itself—all that it perceives is from either an internal or external sense that provides the datum from which our intellectual responses are derived.

In this sense, Hume is a precursor of the associationist movement of Alexander Bain in psychology and the behaviorist counterpart that followed in this country. It would be unfair to call him a sensationist, pure and simple; however, he does emphasize the origin of the cognitive process in the realm of impressions. This became the fundamental starting point for the entire empirical movement. The nature of the knowing mind contributes nothing to experience. Hume claims that the reason we arrange our impressions in certain ways is because of habit or custom; that is, through the ways we are taught and the associations our memories make through past experience. As the result, our understanding is no richer than our experience and the limitations of our experience will in turn affect directly our conceptual capacities. Thus there is no need to postulate a mind or self in some metaphysical sense in order to provide a source of unity and integration to our experience. Such unity is brought about, according to Hume, by the perpetual and habitual ways we are taught to relate our perceptions. All perceptions are distinct and separate. Here is the positivistic view of knowledge that has so greatly influenced the epistemological notions of our own time.

Hume's stress is upon the particular and the specific; universal judgments are made when we perceive similarities among particulars and as the consequence assign names to the common characteristics of separate perceptions that appear similar. When we use the term horse, in a generic sense, we are merely attributing the common attributes we perceive as we observe this or that particular horse. This is in contrast to Plato's idea of a metaphysical realm of universals in his philosophical "realism." Hume, a philosophical "nominalist," views universals as a convenient way of denoting like perceptions. Hume is not only skeptical about the objective reality of "forms" or "universals," but he is also uncertain about the objective reality of the external world because, in his view, we can only be certain about the psychological reality of our impressions. We can only suppose that the source of our impressions is an external world, in some sense, "out there." If we do assume that it "exists," we can never be certain about its nature. The point of focus, for our study, is that the source of all our knowledge comes only from experience. Hume's stress upon a subjective or psychological epistemology and his rejection of the metaphysics of "things," for all practical purposes becomes a "metaphysics of knowledge," as Windelband points out.[13]

The impact of Hume's skepticism affects three areas of belief and thought that relate to "secularist" views of reality. (1) Beliefs about morality and ethics; (2) Beliefs about God; (3) Beliefs about the Self.

(1) His views regarding the sources for morality are consistent with his general posture of uncertainty about any realm of knowledge. For him, moral judgments develop because of social necessity. There is no place in his under-

standing for a priori ethical obligations or for absolute moral ideas or principles. The moral sense resides in a socially conditioned moral sentiment that finds satisfaction and pleasure in what is deemed good and displeasure in what is felt to be bad. Hume states, ". . . morality is determined by sentiment. It defines virtue to be *whatever mental action or quality gives to a spectator* the pleasing sentiment of approbation; and vice the contrary." [14] Therefore, the problem of morality becomes a matter of determining what action produces within men feelings of approbation and sentiments of displeasure. By this method we can determine the basis for the moral life. Morality is no longer a question for speculative philosophy or metaphysical affirmation, but is a study for empirical investigation. The modern ring of this approach is striking as one observes the essentially phenomenal or descriptive approaches to moral behavior within the social sciences as they attempt to be value-free. This is in contrast to that tradition within moral philosophy that deduces ethical norms from a priori moral principles. Hume urges a "reformation in all moral disquisitions;" and a rejection of "every system of ethics, however subtle and ingenious, which is not founded on fact and observation." [15] This does not mean that Hume has no ethical point of view; rather, he attempts to establish a rationale for defending the preference of certain types of behavior over others on the grounds of their social usefulness.

For example, he argues that such virtues as benevolence "promote the interests of our species, and bestow happiness on human society;" [16] likewise the principles of equity and justice find approval because of their beneficial consequences for the individual and the society. Because these virtues appeal to the moral sentiments of men due to their practical utility, they are justified as worthy of man's approval. Hume endeavors to establish a posteriori that utility is the sole source and reason for the high regard we pay to the virtues of justice, honor, allegiance and chastity. He further argues that the praise and approbation we give to utility is "inseparable from all of the other social virtues, humanity, generosity, charity, affability, lenity, mercy and moderation." "In a word," he adds, "it is a foundation of the chief part of morals, which has a reference to mankind and our fellow creatures." [17] It is doubtful that Hume adequately establishes the legitimacy of the claim for such virtues upon our lives on a purely empirical basis, but it is an attempt to predicate the ground for morality upon human experience independent of pure reason, intuition or revealed truth. This casts the question of what is good or bad, right or wrong within social experience that is empirically accessible. The issue here is not whether Hume establishes adequately his claim empirically; it is only to point out that he assumes that a "moral science" is possible based upon the assumption that man is motivated by self-interest and social necessity and that conformity to these demands will bring him pleasure. John Stuart Mill's utilitarianism was indebted to Hume's views. Mill also found justification for the principle of utility, as a moral claim, because of its relationship to the "moral sentiment"—a notion that has been central in a great deal of humanistic thought since that time.

(2) There are two aspects of Hume's beliefs about God and religion upon which I would like to focus. (a) Hume's views concerning the origin of religion, and (b) his attack upon all attempts to justify a belief in God.

(a) In *The Natural History of Religion,* he finds no basis for attributing man's religious response to nature and the world or to some "original instinct" or "primary impression of nature." It is interesting to note that he finds some natural basis for such virtues as self-love, affection between man and woman, and love of progeny as universal responses among persons. But such is not the story regarding the origin or evolution of religion because some people have been discovered to have no belief in an invisible intelligent power or agent. Furthermore, Hume contends, when such beliefs are affirmed, there seldom is agreement about the nature of the powers that allegedly exist. Religion arises along with other superstitions because of man's defenseless state and ignorance about the forces of nature. In those peoples that embrace polytheism, the ideas about the relationship of the gods to man and nature do not arise as the result of man's reflection about nature, but, rather, as the result of the contingencies of nature over which man has no control. Such fears elicit supernatural explanations for causes that men neither know nor understand. Hume has nothing but contempt for religious beliefs that link superstitions with belief in a sovereign deity that is infinitely superior to mankind, because such beliefs degrade man and lead him to acts of self-mortification and passive suffering that he believes to be virtuous. Hume observes a curious admixture of anthropomorphism and philosophical reflection in many developed religions, not the least of which is Christianity. Curiously enough he admires those who endeavor to establish belief in a Supreme Creator through rational means, but he has great difficulty in accepting the vulgar interpretations and understanding of most men. Look at the religions of mankind, he suggests, and see how they pervert the truths of their faith.

Examine the religious principles which have, in fact, prevailed in the world. You will scarcely be persuaded that they are anything but sick men's dreams; or perhaps will regard them more as the playsome whimseys of monkeys in human shape, than the serious, positive,

41

dogmatical asseverations of a being, who dignifies himself with the name of rational.[18]

(b) Regarding Hume's attack upon all attempts to provide either a rational or empirical justification for a belief in God, there is an ambivalence in his thought. Throughout the *Dialogues Concerning Natural Religion,* Hume attacks all of the major traditional arguments for the existence of God in the person of Philo, the philosophical inquirer; yet, in the end of the *Dialogues* he finds, of all of the arguments, the argument from design, the most plausible though not convincing. Hume's skepticism pervades his total thought. He cannot fly to revealed truth nor can he rely on his own intuitions as a satisfactory ground for certainty. "To be a philosophic sceptic is, in a man of letters," he believes, "the first and most essential step towards being a sound, believing Christian." [19] If this be so, then what is the ground for belief in God? I agree with Henry Aiken,[20] when he suggests that Hume was neither an atheist nor a believer, a materialist nor a naturalist in the traditional meaning of these terms. He was skeptical of all attempts to establish a belief about the ultimate nature of things. His emphasis in his epistemology upon custom and habit as affecting the ways by which we relate our impressions of the external world to each other probably applies to matters of religious faith as well. Since he finds no necessary cause for religious belief, belief in God remained an enigma and an inexplicable mystery beyond human cognitive powers to understand. This is illustrated in the *Dialogues* when Philo agrees with Demea, the Orthodox Christian, who believes that God is beyond human understanding. Thus any philosophic attempt to place God's existence within a rational framework of meaning is both futile and unnecessary. Likewise Hume's denial of miracles in the last part of the *Enquiry* and his disbelief in immortality, as well as his disavowal of the necessity for any religious claim to be the foundation for an ethical system, indicate his thoroughgoing skepticism. His attempt to base morality on a humanistic foundation falsifies any argument that would make religious belief an essential part of the moral life or as providing a serious claim upon the life of man.

Nevertheless, the crucial blow to the rational attempt to justify a belief in God is his attack upon the causal argument for God's existence that had been the basic "proof" for God's existence from the time of Aristotle on. It was assumed that something could not come from nothing; therefore, there must be a First Cause or Prime Mover that exists behind all that is. Such an affirmation was not the result of an empirical observation but was believed to be a logical necessity; it could not be thought otherwise. In addition, it was believed to be substantiated in experience because when we observe an effect, we usually find a cause for that which occurs. Therefore, it was assumed that there could be no effect at any time that was not preceded by a cause.

Hume, on the other hand, both in his *Treatise of Human Nature,* his first philosophic work, and in his later and more mature essay, *An Enquiry Concerning Human Understanding,* as well as in the *Dialogues,* laboriously shows that there is no logically necessary relationship between cause and effect. We make these connections through custom and habit. The relationship is one of contiguity and not continuity. He says,

> When we look about us towards external objects, and consider the operation of causes, we are never able, in a single instance, to discover any power of necessary connexion; any quality, which bind the effect to the cause, and renders the one an infallible consequence of the other. We only find, that the one does actually,

43

in fact, follow the other ... Consequently there is not, in any single particular of cause and effect, any thing which can suggest the idea of power or necessary connexion.[21]

And in another passage he says,

This idea of connexion among events arises from a number of similar instances which occur of the constant conjunction of these events ... This connexion ... which we feel in the mind, this customary transition of the imagination from one object to its usual attendant, is the sentiment or impression from which we form the idea or power of necessary connexion.[22]

(3) Not only does Hume undercut the logical basis for a metaphysics of causality but he also challenges the identity of the self as traditionally conceived. Descartes held that the most indubitable reality of all experience is the existence of a self. His famous statement, *cogito ergo sum,* predicates the existence of a metaphysical self that makes the very process of doubt possible because if there is a doubt there must be a doubter. Hume does not find it necessary to postulate existence of a self as the unifier of experience and applies his general agnosticism to what had been generally believed to be the most self-evident of all primary intuitions. Hume recognizes that the problem of the self is one of the most complex and difficult philosophical questions and acknowledges the inadequacy of his uncertainty about the self. For example, in the "Appendix" to his *Treatise,* he shares this uneasiness about his attempt to deal with this problem. Nonetheless, Hume holds the position, consistent with his total philosophy, that the senses give us no more assurance that there exists behind the flow of our perceptions and feelings a self, than these experi-

44

ences can provide for us a sense of the reality of a "substance" or "essence" that exists in some metaphysical way within or outside of the world beyond our perceptions.

If we ask Hume, what is the thinking self? he replies, "The mind is a kind of theatre, where several perceptions successively make their appearance; pass, re-pass, glide away, and mingle in an infinite variety of postures and situations. There is properly no *simplicity* in it at one time, nor *identity* in different; whatever natural propension we may have to imagine that simplicity and identity." [23] If the existence of the self and the external world cannot be known directly, then what is the basis for such beliefs? Hume answers that we imagine there is a self that unifies and makes our perceptions coherent; thus, there appears to be more regularity in our perceptions than what we actually perceive. Thus we "feign some new and intelligible principles" that connect what we perceive together. Such notions as *soul, self* or *substance* are unwarranted postulates. The tendency "to confound identity with relation" is so great, that we are apt to imagine something unknown and mysterious to explain what appears to be the unity of the knowing self or the connection between what is perceived.[24] In the final analysis, Hume cannot find any theory that gives a satisfactory explanation for the process by which the successive perceptions in thought and consciousness are united.[25] Whether or not current nerve-net theories of consciousness would satisfy his demands is an open question; perhaps they would because Hume's philosophy tends to be reductionistic. Therefore, the reduction of consciousness to a neurological phenomenon might have satisfied the empirical demand he tries to place upon the examination of all phenomena. In any event, Hume can find no answer. From his perspective, it is not necessary to answer these speculative questions about the nature of the knowing mind in order to function in the world. In a sense, his practical and utilitarian philosophy takes over and is applicable to the limitations of his theoretical agnosticism. We can only assume there is an external world that corresponds to our perceptions and that the relations between our perceptions are valid because such assumptions are operationally useful. Parenthetically, I might add that the reason many scientists find metaphysical issues irrelevant is because answers to these questions are not necessary to move ahead in the scientific and technological enterprise. To be sure there is the theoretical aspect of science that provides a model and system upon which applied efforts can be based. However, the attractiveness of the theory, in the final analysis, is in the fact that it is *useful in solving problems.* Hume's interest in the *how* of things, rather than the *why* of things is a part of the transition from the ancient to the modern worldview.

It is dangerous to trace modern views to a source two hundred years removed from the present day, but I think certain of Hume's ideas are parallel to the modern temper found among intellectuals in our time. Just to mention a few of these: his anti-metaphysical bias; his conviction that all knowledge comes from impressions that are stimulated from without or within; his attraction to a psychological and sociological understanding of the roots of religious beliefs; his consistent skepticism about knowing anything for certain; his utilitarian arguments for the necessity of ethics; his attempt to base primary ethical responses in feelings of approbation and disapprobation; his uncertainty about the underlying nature of man; and his stress upon the importance of methodology in human inquiry.

Auguste Comte's Positivism

Auguste Comte (1798-1857), one of the most impressive minds of the 19th century, attempted to develop a philosophy that would be adequate for all time and a method that would provide knowledge that would be "sure" and "certain," that is, *positif.* His model was that of the physical sciences and he assumed that the phenomena of human thought and society could be studied in a way analogous to the examination of the inorganic and organic worlds of nature. He rejected traditional religious beliefs, including a belief in God, during his adolescent years, and spent his life developing a social philosophy devoid of conventional religious trappings. His passion was to develop a system of thought that would give the same assurances of "certainty" that revealed religion had provided for mankind; hence there was a "religious" and "messianic" tone to his work that evolved into a Positive Religion of Humanity that would appeal to both the intellect and the emotions through which a moral and mental regeneration would emerge giving rise to political expression that would benefit all mankind. Philosophy and polity were considered inseparable. In fact, he hoped some day to preach his gospel of Positivism from the pulpit of Notre Dame. In 1848 Comte organized the Positivist Society. Originally, it was a political discussion and action group and soon developed into a quasi-religious movement seeking its own disciples. The movement spread to England where Richard Congreve was its leading exponent. Being a Positivist meant more than believing some abstract philosophic system; rather, it meant a commitment to a philosophy of action and renewal. The period in which Comte lived was one of upheaval and unrest and it was his conviction that old social organizations were obsolete and new structures must replace them. This renewal should not happen in any haphazard way but through a thorough understanding and knowledge of how social structures develop. Social theories, he believed, cannot be spun out of the head—social processes must be observed and the dynamics of social controls understood.

As the father of sociology, Comte wanted to be as rigorous as possible in his application of scientific methods in order to explain the laws of social development that could serve as a basis for anticipating the social character of future societies. This was no small undertaking. It involved the classification of all of the sciences and the development of a kind of "unified field theory" that would encompass all of human experience. He argued that philosophy must shed its metaphysical and speculative endeavors and become a philosophy of science. In that way its theories can be tested. The encompassing character of Positive Philosophy is well stated by M. Pierce Laffite, one of Comte's more able interpreters, when he says that Positivism is:

> ... a general doctrine providing common and universal rules for the direction of the world, man and society ... a doctrine which comprehends all that it is given to us to know, and which in its totality contains parts so well connected and so consonant with each other, and so complete, that nothing is left to change, no problem is left without solution, and everyone knows in all circumstances what we must think.[26]

Comte's philosophy had a historical, present and futuristic emphasis. Current social scientific developments in general systems analysis, alternative futures, cybernetic social engineering, and the like are attempts to shape social patterns in accord with rationally and empirically determined laws. Regarding Comte's influence, Gertrud Lenzer observes, "at times it is uncanny to read announcements that often recall almost verbatim the words of their common mentor and ancestor."[27] One of the intriguing aspects of his thought, that is most relevant to the development of a secular humanistic view of man and his world, is Comte's analysis of the evolution of human thought from primitive to scientific or positive forms, and his attempt to develop a comprehensive understanding of all phenomena according to the laws of nature. Comte's positive philosophy is one of the most ambitious attempts in western thought to build a society upon a scientific basis and at the same time be responsive to humanistic goals and ideas. At many points, his Religion of Humanity is strikingly similar to Karl Marx's ideal society where ostensibly the goal is the realization of the full potential of every person.

Comte suggests there are three stages in the evolution of man's understanding of his relationship to the world: (1) The theological stage; (2) The metaphysical stage; and (3) The positive stage.

(1) The theological stage was man's earliest reflective attempt to arrange his experiences in some orderly fashion. On this level, man sought to understand the nature of reality including first and final causes, and because he did not understand natural law and natural processes he believed that all phenomena are the result ultimately of supernatural causes. Theological speculation reached its highest level in monotheism which assumed that all that occurs is the result of the action and purpose of a single Being. Thus these beliefs gave unity and order to reality and had a very practical function as well because through such faith men "could obtain confidence, and therefore courage, only from above, and through the illusion of an illimitable power residing there ... could on any occasion afford them irresistible aid." [28] In its practical function, theology provided a similar function as the "chimeras" of astrology and alchemy. Theologians tried to maintain the reality of an objective source for their "theological synthesis" that was in fact based exclusively upon man's "affective nature"; "this was the cause for its original supremacy and its ultimate decline." [29] Comte attributes religious beliefs to a subjective source when he says, "In theological systems the objective

basis was supplied by spontaneous belief in a supernatural Will ... Now, whatever the degree of reality attributed to these fictions, they all proceeded from a subjective source." [30] In another passage, he calls them, "spontaneous fictions admitting of no proof." [31] These are strikingly familiar statements about religious beliefs emanating from positivistic philosophical circles in our own time.

(2) The metaphysical stage provided an intermediary role between the theological and the scientific or positive philosophy. Due to the fact that the theological and positive world-views are so different and because human understanding is so slow in developing, the metaphysical perspective provided a useful function of transition. In the final analysis, the metaphysical state is only a modification of earlier theological views since it affirms the reality of abstract forces or principles at work in nature as an attempt to explain the uniqueness of a species, for example, or the teleological function of nature itself. Since metaphysical systems are more abstract and more intellectually sophisticated than the more primitive forms of theological speculation, they are more amenable to a naturalistic explanation of the world and thus prepare the soil for the acceptability of a scientific or positive explanation of nature's ways. Comte argues that metaphysics is to be preferred to the anthropomorphism of theology, but it is still a speculative system and falls short of the demands of positive philosophy for evidence. Comte makes only passing references to theology and metaphysics and devotes most of his attention to the development of his positive philosophy—the mature way of looking at the world.

(3) What are the basic tenets of positive philosophy? First of all, Comte assumes the adequacy of the scientific method as appropriate for investigating any phenomena. At the outset of his discussion of Positive Philosophy he says,

In the final, the positive, state, the mind has given over the vain search after absolute notions, the origin and destination of the universe, and the causes of phenomena, and applies itself to the study of their laws—that is, their invariable relations of succession and resemblance. Reasoning and observation, duly combined, are the means of this knowledge.[32]

Since metaphysical assertions about ultimate causes are unknowable, the business of philosophy is to analyze the "circumstances of phenomena" in accord with the laws according to which they function. This principle applies to all phenomena including the laws of mental and social development.

Parenthetically, I am reminded of a student, majoring in one of the social sciences, walking up to me on the campus a number of years ago and saying, "How is the Head of the Department of Unknowables today?" She was reflecting Comte's positive philosophy without knowing it.

Comte assumes that by knowing and understanding the laws of physical nature and the laws of mental and social growth, we can develop one general system that will enable us to understand all aspects of the whole. The crucial point is Comte's *faith* in the principle that invariable laws can be applied to all realms of experience and that if we knew enough about these laws we could understand the present and anticipate the future. Earlier, Francis Bacon suggested the appropriateness of the inductive method of understanding nature, but did not go so far as to *deify* his method as the only way to understand all phenomena. Comte was nearer to *scientism* (claiming the scientific method as the only meaningful approach) than science, because the spirit of science dictates an openness to other dimensions of meaning that cannot be encapsulated within a single system of understanding.

Comte's observations about the advantages of positive philosophy over other methods is of importance. He points out that positive philosophy provides the only means of demonstrating the "logical laws of the mind" based upon physiological functions, what he calls "cerebral physiology." The advantages of the experimental method are superior to other approaches that would rely on subjective reports of how the mind functions. As difficult as it is to stand external to one's own mind, positive philosophy provides the method and approach that enables one to look objectively at how the intellect functions in accordance with the rules of nature. Also, he believes that positive philosophy has a constructive effect upon education. Comte believes that education had been too greatly dominated by theological and metaphysical speculative disciplines; he argues that such training perhaps has value in the earlier years, but it must now give way to positive training that is more "conformable to our own time and needs." Since all of the sciences are "branches from one trunk," it is important for a student to "obtain general positive conceptions of all the classes of natural phenomena." Specialties, he suggests, can be deferred until the student has a grounding in the fundamental laws that govern the natural order. When this is achieved, the student can draw into a meaningful synthesis of knowledge the underlying structure of reality that will be applicable to the particular area of special knowledge he wishes to pursue. For example, any adequate study of physical bodies must be understood from both their physical and chemical components.

All of the sciences, he argues, are interrelated. Thus Comte seeks "the elucidation of the respective sciences by their combination." [33] As I have pointed out, Comte's interests do not end with the physical sciences but he extends his method to the social sciences as well, particularly sociology of which he is considered the founder. He seeks a solid basis for social organization and views the application of scientific methods to social problems as the only way for a society to raise itself out of intellectual and social anarchy. He endeavors to adapt, by analogy, the nature of physical organisms to a study of the organic character of social structures. He is not *Gestalt* in his approach; rather, he insists that social organisms must be seen in the light of their constituent elements and unique history. As in the case of the application of the scientific method to organic structures, the danger is that of reductionism and the failure to recognize that the whole is greater than the sum of its parts. His contribution is his insight that historical analysis is another way to observe how societies develop. At the same time he warns that such approaches must be always subject "to the philosophical conditions imposed by the positive spirit of sociology." [34]

His faith in positive philosophy is further illustrated in his belief that it will unite reason, imagination and feeling and provide an integrated basis for man to find fulfillment in his world. His task is impressive: to understand the dynamics of physical and social development and to make these laws coherent, through logical and mathematical formulations, so that they can be applied to practical life. Additional evidence of the contemporary nature of Comte's philosophy is his view that positive philosophy deals with reality and at the same time is useful because it is certain and precise. He saw these attributes as sufficient to provide man with "spiritual direction." He recognizes that man has emotional as well as intellectual needs, and as we have pointed out earlier, Comte attempts to build a system that will bring man's rational capacities into a coherent relationship with his affective nature.

Not only was Comte's philosophy thoroughly secular or

naturalistic, but it was also humanistic. The Religion of Humanity (he writes about this in the upper case), toward which positive philosophy aspires is motivated by human love based upon the needs of all men. In Comte's emphasis upon love and service to all mankind, he attempts to provide the same goals taught by traditional western religions. All material values, he suggests, are subordinate to human well being and the social and moral growth of every person. The ideal society would be one in which progress and the development of order would be under the influence of love. Life has intrinsic value and becomes "a continuous and earnest act of worship." Without apology, Comte affirms that "Positivism becomes, in the true sense of the word, a Religion; the only religion which is real and complete; destined therefore to replace all imperfect and provisional systems resting on the primitive basis of theology." [35] The priests of Humanity are the philosophers of the future and will occupy a position of unparalleled dignity. Reason, imagination and feeling will be brought into unison and will affect constructively the conditions of practical life. All effort will be directed toward "the elevation of man." He says,

> Science, Poetry, Morality, will be devoted to the study, the praise, and the love of Humanity, in order that under their combined influence, our political action may be more unremittingly given to her service ... With such a mission, Science acquires a position of unparalleled importance, as the sole means through which we come to know the nature and conditions of the Great Being, the worship of whom should be the distinctive feature of our whole life.[36]

Here the secular and the humanistic join hands in a perfect marriage. All faith is placed in science, its objectivity and quantitatively precise methods. The future lies in the hands of men of science; the elite is born displacing the old priesthood of traditional religion. A new Religion of Humanity is the hope for the future—any other hopes placed in other forms of knowledge are misplaced and are remnants of the superstitious past from which we have been delivered. Though present day forms of science are more modest in their claims, the layman finds the data of scientific inquiry impressive and the practical usefulness of exploring unknown areas of the universe in outer space inspiring. If the expenditure of time, money and energy were any indication of where our civilization places its hopes for the future and are indicative of the gods we worship, science and technology would be high on the agenda of our commitments. The wars and holocausts since the 19th century have tempered the overly zealous who would place all of their faith in science, but the remnants of humanistic faith that places knowledge only attained through rational human inquiry, as the source for our redemption, still remains. To this question we will return later in our comments about the faith of secular humanism. This faith is epitomized in the positive philosophy of Auguste Comte. His faith and spirit is far from dead!

Along with a large body of secular humanists of our own day, Comte affirms, "Accepting the truths of science, it [positive morality] teaches that we must look to our own unremitting activity for the only providence by which the rigor or our destiny can be alleviated." [37] It would be absurd to assume that human activity and effort in solving our problems is irrelevant; on the other hand, there may be other sources that can elevate the human spirit and bring about a condition for the wholeness of man than that provided within the narrow understanding of reality that positive philosophy provides. My objection is to Comte's dogmatism and that the only path to the resolution of the human dilemma is through science.

In the final analysis, for Comte, as well as for many

others who find his positive philosophy attractive, theological and metaphysical questions are irrelevant. The ultimate nature of reality can be set aside because this question is not accessible to the methods of scientific investigation. Comte reflects this popular contemporary view when he says, "The true Positive spirit consists in substituting the study of the invariable Laws of phenomenon for that of their so-called Causes ... in a word, in studying the *How* instead of the *Why*." [38]

Charles Darwin's Naturalism

As Hume was the watershed separating the certainties of rationalism from the skepticism of empiricism, so was Darwin the dividing line between non-empirical affirmations about the origin and development of nature and the empirically substantiated conviction that nature has evolved over a period of billions of years. The notion that nature is the product of continuous development was not entirely new, but it had been defended primarily upon a theoretical basis; it was Darwin who gave it a substantial empirical ground.

His father was a physician. Darwin considered being a physician at one time in his development, as well as a clergyman, but his insatiable curiosity about nature's ways led him into the natural sciences. He came under the influence of some of the leading naturalists of his day while attending the universities of Edinburgh and Cambridge. Early in his studies he was intrigued by William Paley's *Natural Theology* and, according to his own testimony, was "charmed and convinced by the long line of argumentation." [39] Paley was a naturalistic philosopher-theologian who argued for a teleological or purposive view of nature and attempted to defend this thesis on rational and empirical grounds. While at Cambridge, Darwin developed an

56

interest in geological studies and, during one of his field trips, found a tropical shell in a gravel bed in the middle of England that fascinated him immeasurably. But the turning point in his life was the invitation by Captain Fitz-Roy to join a world-wide scientific expedition on the H.M.S. Beagle. This experience, Darwin observes, was my "first real training or education of mind." [40] For the most part, he found the professors and their lectures in Scotland and England tiring and boring.

While on the voyage of the Beagle he read two volumes of Sir Charles Lyell's, *The Principles of Geology,* which suggested that geological studies warrant the postulate that the age of the earth goes back aeons in time. Darwin saw the application of this principle to the development of living things as well. While on the Beagle, he carefully kept a journal of his explorations in the Galapagos Archipelago and other places he visited; his letters to his colleagues in England were so impressive that some of them were read before the Philosophical Society at Cambridge. The experience on the Beagle provided him a five year period for reflection and observation. Darwin reports, "As soon as I had become, in the year 1837 or 1838, convinced that species were mutable production, I could not avoid the belief that man must come under the same law." [41] Thus the theory of man's evolution was conceived, but not yet born. In 1838 he read T. R. Malthus, *Essay on the Principle of Population,* that helped solidify his theory that in the struggle for existence favorable variations would tend to be preserved and unfavorable ones destroyed resulting in the formation of new species. Twenty-one years later (1859) his great work, *On the Origin of Species by Means of Natural Selection,* was published. Here the famous principles of "natural selection" and "survival of the fit" were affirmed and the story of organic evolution was sustained by observational data. If Darwin had only applied these principles to lower forms of life, his theories would probably have not created the furor that followed, particularly in religious circles. In the opening paragraph of *The Descent of Man* he states that he considered not publishing his notes on the origin of man because "I thought that I should thus only add to the prejudices against my views." [42]

Nonetheless, when he applied these principles to the evolution of man, he challenged a central idea, sacred to both the Jewish and Christian traditions for thousands of years, that man had been created by a special act of God. Generally speaking, Jews and Christians based their convictions about special creation upon the Genesis account that included not only man, but other species as well. It was widely held that species were permanent and immutable. As the result of Darwin's theory, man was displaced from the center of the creative process. Darwin did for biology what Copernicus had done for cosmology; he removed man from the center of God's universe and placed him within the natural cosmic order. The implications of Darwin's views are clear: The story of creation no longer need be considered as the result of God's creative act of love, but as the result of fortuitous circumstance and the ability of the species to survive; nature has its own economy, its own way of doing things; it need not be explained by attributing its natural processes to some metaphysical principle or theological agent; nature *natures* in accord with its own laws; and the task of man is to understand, through observation and analysis, nature's ways.

As in the case of Frances Bacon, David Hume, and Auguste Comte, Darwin had "no need for the God hypothesis" to explain natural processes. He rejected Paley's teleological world-view, broke away from the Church of England and was an agnostic in his later years. Darwin, like so many natural scientists in our day, was not anti-religious; he was intellectually areligious, that is, he did not see the relevance of religious beliefs to an understanding of man and nature.

At the same time, he had to explain man's uniqueness; and this was the subject for his very important essay, *The Descent of Man,* that appeared in 1871. He wrote this work with some trepidation, but felt that he must spell out the full implications of his theory of evolution as it pertained to man. It was clear to Darwin that "species are the modified descendants of other species," [43] including man. He presents data supporting his claim that man has been constructed on the same general model as other vertebrate animals, and argues that the variations within species are caused by the same general laws that operate within lower animals. Applying uniformity of a causal biological connection between lower animals and man is not as disturbing to anti-evolutionists, who advocate man's inherent uniqueness as a rational being, as when a correlative relationship is established between man's physical, and mental or spiritual nature. Darwin stuck with a biological model of man and endeavored to explain what appears to be man's distinctively human capacities as due to both physical and environmental causes.

How does Darwin attempt to explain man's "uniqueness"? He grants that the difference between the mental powers of the lowest savage and the highest ape is enormous, but that this does not warrant the admission of other than a naturalistic explanation for the difference. Darwin believes that there were numberless gradations, from one level to another, in the evolutionary process; thus, it is fruitless to try and explain at what point in that process the mental powers, within animals or men, began to appear. Men and other primates hold many things in common—intuitions and sensations, passions and emotions. Both are deceitful, revengeful, jealous, suspicious, grateful, generous; they reason, deliberate, choose, feel, wonder and the like, but "in different degrees." [44] Darwin further describes man's conceptual capacities, his self-conscious experiences, his language, his sense of beauty, and his moral and religious experience and then concludes,

> There can be no doubt that the difference between the mind of the lowest man and that of the highest animal is immense ... nevertheless the *difference in mind* between man and the higher animals, great as it is, certainly *is one of degree and not of kind* ... the senses and intuitions, the various emotions and faculties, such as love, memory, attention, curiosity, imitation, reason, etc., of which man boasts may be found in an incipient, or even sometimes in a well-developed condition in the lower animals.[45] (Italics mine.)

Regarding the moral sense, Darwin admits that this may be the best illustration of man's uniqueness, but in the final analysis he attributes the concern for the good of others and oneself as developing out of social instincts. He says, "the social instincts .. with the aid of active intellectual powers and the effects of habit, naturally lead to the golden rule ... and this lies at the foundation of morality." [46]

The contemporaneity of this image of man, as a product of his biological and social environments, is striking as is the belief that knowledge of these influences upon the individual's development will provide an adequate conceptual framework for understanding man's evolution and development.

A few observations about Darwin's scientific and philosophical perspective: First and foremost Darwin was a biologist and used a biological model to explain all forms of life, including humankind. Thus, all of man's capacities must exist, in their incipient stages, in lower forms of life. His unwillingness to admit a *qualitative* distinction between men and the lower animals is confirmed by his statement that the difference is "one of degree and not of kind." This supports his essentially biological predisposition. As a biologist he could not afford to recognize a qualitative difference between men and animals, because this would have left the door open for the theologian or metaphysician to explain a *difference in kind* by postulating the existence of a *soul, psyche,* or *self* as the differentiating principle that provides a rationale for man's uniqueness. I am sure that Darwin felt that his insistence upon a *quantitative* rather than *qualitative* difference was not a predilection, but that the evidence supported his views. The issue is not closed; the argument about man's fundamental nature continues. The present scientific tendency to quantify all data leads inevitably to a reductionism that distorts the nature of that which is being analyzed. It is difficult to fit man, a minded organism, into simply a biological and social model. Nevertheless, Darwin's attempt to explain man as the product of a biological and social process provided a model for the study of man that has been pervasive since his time. Darwin, in a sense, completes the search for a naturalistic foundation for the explanation of man without the traditional forms of metaphysical and theological support. Of course, naturalism is a metaphysical point of view; in this discourse, we have been identifying metaphysics with the predominant strains of philosophical idealism and realism that characterized much of western philosophic thought until the 16th century.

Secondly, Darwin introduced a genetic approach to physical and social development. By genetic I mean the attempt to trace the evolution of phenomena to their origins or genesis. The influence of this approach to the study of social phenomena is apparent in the disciplines of sociology and anthropology. There is little question that tracing the evolutionary development of phenomena is helpful and informative, but the problem in reducing phenomena to their origins, is to avoid the fallacy of reductionism. Students are often lured into the genetic fallacy when they say that religion is "nothing-but" superstition, or man is "nothing-but" a bio-chemical higher organism. To trace the origins and evolutionary development of any facet of human experience is illuminating; but does the genetic approach explain adequately the experience in question? Without doubt many of our civilized forms of expression have had primitive origins, but to suggest that all present and more refined forms of human experience are, in the final analysis, nothing-but the form out of which it developed is to do an injustice to the richness and full meaning of that experience. Aesthetic, moral and religious experiences are cases in point. Or to suggest that the utilitarian value of a belief warrants its acceptance and affirms its value in a given time and place in history, does not justify its truth claim or the objective basis for the meaning it provided at another time. Nonetheless, the genetic approach to phenomena, from earlier to more advanced forms, is very much a part of the present academic and intellectual scene and often serves as a way of avoiding the problem of the validity of the truth-claim that was made for a particular experience. The phenomenological approach, when essentially descriptive, is one of the current and very popular forms of this perspective.

Third, Darwin's emphasis upon the "struggle for existence" and "natural selection" has been translated into negative views of human nature, namely, that man by nature is inclined toward survival at any cost. It is doubtful that Darwin had any intention that his naturalistic understanding of man, as a part and product of nature, would be so interpreted, but in the popular mind allusions to the "survival of the fit" and "struggle for existence" have been used to support the "naturalness" of competition and the survival ethic in business and economic life. As "nature is red in tooth and claw," it is argued, so is man by nature the same. In its more gross forms this "empirical fact" has been affirmed as the basis for the argument that capitalism is superior to other economic systems because it fits man's "natural" competitive tendencies. Darwin should not be blamed for this misuse of his views, though it can be understood how such extrapolations could be made from Darwin's *Origins of Species,* if one had not read *The Descent of Man* that places man within a social context.

However, the important point to note, for our study, is Darwin's major impact upon contemporary man's view of himself and his world in naturalistic and secular terms. To a large extent he was responding to the uncritical and popular supernaturalism of his time, just as Comte, Hume and others were reacting to the religious naiveté of the popular religion of their day. It may be that today we are confronted with a new dogma that is as uncritical of a completely naturalistic attempt to explain all of human experience as was the supernaturalism against which the movement originally reacted. Perhaps the type of naturalism that followed the 16th century needs to be challenged once again. The dogma rejected by one generation is often replaced by a dogma of another generation. By dogma, I mean an unwillingness to examine, or even seriously entertain, any claim for truth that does not fit into one's own methodological approach to knowledge. In other words, the method is the message. All of us who are teachers have encountered the bright science major who has been so inculcated with the superiority of the scientific method that no other approach to reality is an intellectual option; he often is as uncritical of the adequacy of the methods he employs as a "scientist" as the student who is a disciple of some form of Yoga.

The reason I have chosen Darwin as the epitome of a naturalistic-scientific view of man and nature is that he endeavored to follow an empirical approach to a study of man more thoroughly than any other scientist prior to his time. At the same time, he did not feel that this degraded man's status. He concludes *The Descent of Man* by placing man at the "summit of the organic scale ... [which] may give him hope for a still higher destiny in the distant future." Nevertheless, with all of his exalted powers, "Man still bears in his bodily frame the indelible stamp of his lowly origin." [47]

Sigmund Freud's Subjectivism

It is not our purpose to present a full scale portrait of Freud's multi-faceted psychology; rather, it is our intent to focus on his views regarding the nature of man and society and how these notions have influenced contemporary secular perspectives that are prevalent today. Without question, Freud is one of the most influential figures of our time in reshaping man's image of himself and explaining the forces that shape his behavior. As the result of the Neo-Freudian movement initiated by Karen Horney, Erich Fromm and others in this country, few orthodox Freudians remain; nevertheless, remnants of his analysis of the dynamics of character formation and its implications for morality and religion linger.

Freud was greatly influenced by Darwin's work and, during his student days, did original research in physiology and anatomy. He became interested in aphasia and the cerebral paralyses of children and, very early in his career, worked with Josef Breur on the problem of hysteria, co-publishing a work with him in 1895. He soon became fascinated with the complexity of psychological phenomena; this study led him away from the customary interests of medicine to the development of psychoanalytic theory with which he is primarily identified. His pioneer work was resisted by most of his colleagues, but his persistence and commitment to truth, as he perceived it, lead to a movement that had far reaching effects throughout the world. As Erich Fromm has pointed out, his ethical relativism did not include his pursuit of truth. Integrity and honesty were the absolutes in his moral consciousness as he tried to be faithful to the full implications of his studies regardless of the consequences. In a day dominated by Victorian attitudes and values such an enterprise was not easy—men of less courage would have succumbed to the prevailing ethos of the time. But such was not the case with Freud.

Freud's analysis of the structure of human personality is very important for our study because, from my view, *what a person thinks about the nature of man will have a profound bearing upon his ethical and religious views.* Freud's background in medicine, particularly anatomy and neurology, is important because he consistently sought a neurological explanation underlying psychological appearances. His unwillingness to abandon physiological presuppositions affected his entire work. Carl Jung, Alfred Adler and others broke away from him because of the inadequacy they found in his predominantly biological orientation.

Also, the physiological model is apparent in Freud's emphasis upon the pleasure principle as the individual seeks release from tensions produced by the desire to find satisfaction for instinctual needs. Thus, an understanding of the instincts and how they function is basic to his views. What follows is a thumbnail sketch of his understanding of the dynamics of personality.[48]

Freud views the instincts as a force or stimulus within man. While man can avoid external stimulii that bring him displeasure, his basic instincts are inescapable. As a consequence, personality is shaped by the innumerable ways man attempts to fulfill and gratify his instinctual needs in an effort to effect a reduction of the tensions they produce.

Such terms as "sublimation," "reaction formation," "repression," "projection," and "transference" are an important part of Freud's vocabulary. Freud sees man as caught between his instinctual nature and the demands society places upon him for conformity.

The id, the seat of the instincts and the original reservoir for all psychic energy, dominates the life of the newborn child. The id lacks any organizing consciousness and, as the dynamo of personality and the generator of the basic energy that flows into the ego, is blind, compulsive and irrational. Contradictory impulses within the id create the inherent ambivalence of man's nature which he cannot escape. As developed in his later writings, Freud identified two of the basic instincts to be self-preservation (ego instincts) and procreation (libido drives) out of which flow the basic energizing forces for behavior. If man does not control the contradiction of his inner life, these forces will erupt and overwhelm him. His work with psychoneurotic patients in World War I, who had traumatic experiences in combat and who relived these experiences in dreams, led Freud to revise his earlier theories. He saw that the tendency to repeat an unsavory experience may be an effort to gain mastery over it and may even be stronger than the pleasure principle itself. About 1920, he added several new views to his instinct theory including the idea that contrasting drives reside within man, namely, the eros or life instinct, and thanatos, the death instinct. Eros tends to unite and bind together while thanatos incites destruction and separation. It is interesting that the death instinct is primarily directed towards the self and not to the outside world. In this view, he does not deny the force of either the instinct for procreation (libido) or the drive for self-preservation (ego); instead, he supplements his earlier analysis of the motivational life of man with the eros/thanatos theory. He characterizes instincts as "tendencies inherent in living substance towards restoring an earlier state of things ... Both classes of instincts, Eros as well as the death instinct," he adds, "would, on this view, have been in operation and working against each other from the origin of life." [49]

The ego gradually emerges out of the id as the individual confronts the demands of "reality." The ego consists of the conscious, the unconscious, that which has been repressed and cannot be called into consciousness at will, and the preconscious, that which is available to awareness. The ego is the executor and endeavors to reconcile the demands of the id, the superego (conscience) and the outside world. The ego serves three masters: the demands of the external world for conformity; the ever present call of the passions and instincts for satisfaction; and the scrutiny of the superego that reflects the demands of social structures, institutions and traditions. The ego, Freud says, "in relationship to the id ... is like a man on horseback, who has to hold check the superior strength of the horse." [50]

The superego represents the standards of the society which have been internalized including parental standards, and the traditional ethical teachings of one's culture. It also includes the standards one sets for himself. The super-ego functions when the self objectifies itself in terms of the expectation it has for itself and the expectations the society makes upon it. Its domination over the ego and its pressing demands to please the external authority, whomever it might be, because of fear of rejection is a part of what becomes the source for moral anxiety within the life of man. Psychoanalysis becomes the medium for freedom from the anxieties created by the guilt ruthlessly imposed upon the individual by a process of character development over which he has had little or no control. Such are the ingredients and the basis of the moral life.

The reason for this brief review of Freud's understanding of the dynamics of the structure of personality development is to show the essentially physiological and instinctual nature of this view of what motivates mankind. He set the pattern for the widespread notion that behavior is motivated, on its deepest level, by need-gratification and some form of self-interest. As the result, the conscious report by the individual of what motivates behavior, particularly when that motivation is attributed to some altruistic or other-directed intent, is often received with skepticism because the definition of man as an instinctually gratifying animal precludes any other interpretation. Thus loving behavior only *appears* to be unselfish because it does not fit the theoretical understanding attributed to man's nature. I recognize that many psychotherapists today take the patient's conscious report of his own motivation seriously, but suspicion of the "purity" of the motivation for kindness and caring still remains. The popular refrain, "I wonder what he wants?" or "What is he up to?" or "What does he want from me?" are not uncommon reactions to acts of human concern. In fact, Freud denies the possibility that one can have disinterested love in another person because of man's own nature. Also, his writings on the meaning of love clearly indicate that one cannot love everyone, nor is love of everyone desirable, because "not all men are worthy of love." [51] He interprets St. Francis of Assisi's love as "exploiting love for the benefit of an inner feeling of happiness." [52]

The view that guilt is caused by the attempt of the superego to regulate forces of the id, so that they will be acceptable to the ego and its relationship to the outside world, places the moral struggle within a psychological and sociological frame of reference. Because man is caught between his instincts and his conscience, liberation can only be found as one frees himself from the tensions that are created by this struggle within himself. As the result, moral problems are seen as essentially psychological problems and the traditional view of ethics as a discipline within moral philosophy is subsumed under psychological and social investigation and analysis. The Neo-Freudian emphasis upon the impact of the culture in character development, coupled with Freud's essentially drive-orientation, reduces moral questions to either an environmental or psychological problem. As the result, the traditional ethical questions about an "objective" right or wrong are aborted and are looked upon as essentially a descriptive problem that can be answered when enough is known about the dynamics of human personality.

I do not want to be misunderstood. There is little question that the environment and the ability of the individual to cope with his basic instincts and needs are of great importance. The issue here is that when moral and ethical questions are dealt with totally within this frame of reference, the historic claim that there are objective moral laws by which a person should live becomes no longer relevant. In its more simple forms, when a child is caught stealing dimes in the cloakroom from the coats of his fellow students, the teacher does not raise the "moral aspects" of the behavior, but helps the child see that if he continues this type of behavior he will be rejected by his peer group; therefore, it is in the child's best interest to stop taking money from other children. The frequent comment, "You aren't making a moral issue out of this, are you?" reflects the attempt to place deviant or unacceptable behavior within an amoral frame of reference. The popular refrain that morality is merely what people agree is right or wrong, good or bad, indicates the impact of Freud's more sophisticated relativism.

My comments are likely to be interpreted as harsh and judgmental. After all, who can claim to know what the right and the good are, assuming there might be an objective moral standard? History is replete with political and religious leaders who claimed they knew what the objective good was and tyrannized their fellow man in the name of some higher law. This is always a problem, but the absence of belief in any ultimate standard by which man should live places the moral question within the framework of a relativism that can justify almost anything to anybody any time. In spite of the dangers of a theologically or metaphysically rooted ethic, seeking what that objective ethical standard is tempers the search with humility, particularly if one refuses to make the claim that he has found it! The same problem applies to any claim for an "objective" truth. We shall return to this question at the end of the essay.

Freud's understanding of the dynamics of character development and its implications for social attitudes is developed in his *Civilization and Its Discontents.* When this essay was being translated, Freud suggested the title, "Man's Discomfort in Civilization," but the title as it now stands prevailed. Its basic theme concerns the irremediable antagonism between the demands of instinct and the restrictions of society. It is his theory of personality writ large. For example, he describes the similarity between the libidinal development of the individual and the process of civilization. He says,

> In most cases this process coincides with that of the *sublimation* [of instinctual aims] ... Sublimation of instinct is an especially conspicuous feature of cultural development; it is what makes it possible for higher psychical activities, scientific, artistic or ideological, to play such an important part in civilized life ... civilization is built up upon a renunciation of instinct.[53]

Since members of a community are mutually threatening to each other, civilized society is in constant threat of being torn apart; therefore, these instinctual passions must be held in check by "psychical reaction-formations." [54] Because "men are not naturally fond of work, and arguments are of no avail against their passions," [55] coercion and "instinctual renunciation" become the means by which civilization is preserved. At the same time man is also motivated by the drive for eros as well as thanatos, so that while civilization checks the impulse to destroy, it also serves the impulse for love and brings individuals together in the form of families, races, communities and nations. What characterizes human nature's ambivalence also marks the ambivalent role that civilization plays as it represents the "struggle between Eros and Death, between the instinct of life and the instinct of destruction ... this struggle is what all life essentially consists of, and the evolution of civilization may therefore be simply described as the struggle for life of the human species." [56] Civilization is not only held in balance by its coercive power, but aggressiveness is inhibited as it is internalized and directed toward the individual's ego. Freud states, "Civilization, therefore, obtains mastery over the individual's dangerous desire for aggression by weakening and disarming it and by setting up an agency within him to watch over it, like a garrison in a conquered city." [57]

Attempts to regulate the moral life, through exhortation or rational argument, is futile. Idealistic ethics only frustrates the individual; hence the demands of the superego must be lowered. The ego is not capable of doing everything the superego might require because the ego does not have unlimited mastery over the id. The command, "to love your neighbor as yourself," is "impossible to fulfill." This "inflation of love" will not eliminate the problem of maintaining a balance between the id and the superego, it will only increase the guilt and tensions within the personality.

71

Man must realistically face his own nature and all Pollyanna types of thinking must go including socialist and humanitarian.

Freud offers no consolation for those who seek an easy remedy for the problems that beset man and society. With the advancement of technology and science, Freud sees the danger of man becoming a "prosthetic God," [58] an illusion as great as any other unwarranted image one might have of himself. Man must face his alienation from himself and his society; he stands alone and ultimately faces his own problems. He states the alienated condition of man well when he says,

For the individual, as for mankind in general, life is hard to endure. The culture in which he shares imposes on him some measure of privation, and other men occasion him a certain degree of suffering ... Add to this the evils that unvanquished nature—he calls Fate—inflict on him. We know already how the individual reacts to the injuries that culture and other men inflict on him: he develops a corresponding degree of resistance against the institutions of this culture, of hostility towards it. But how does he defend himself against the supremacy of nature, of fate, which threatens him, as it threatens all? [59]

Many people, Freud points out, turn to faith in benevolent Providence which will not permit the individual to be the mere plaything of blind natural forces, or be the victim, in the end, of the injustices of this life. In addition, religious sanctions are given to prevailing social norms and standards so that man believes that what happens is not fortuitous but fits into some wider purpose or scheme. Combined with this view of religion, as a compensatory response to a reality man cannot face, is Freud's application of the Oedipus myth to an understanding of the psychological roots of religious belief. Simply stated, Freud argues that man cannot stand rejection; therefore, he projects a father, more powerful than any earthly father, into the nature of things, to protect him and allay his anxiety in the face of an unpredictable future. Freud says,

> Psychoanalysis has made us aware of the intimate connection between the father complex and the belief in God, and has taught us that the personal God is *psychologically* nothing other than a magnified father; it shows us every day how young people lose their religious faith as soon as the father's authority collapses. We thus recognize the root of religious need as lying in the parental complex." [60]

This is the illusory character of religion; it is not necessarily error, that is, a contradiction of fact; rather, it is derived from men's wishes and "approaches psychiatric delusion." Regarding religious doctrines, Freud states that they "are all illusions, they do not admit of proof, and no one can be compelled to consider them to be as true or believe in them ... Of the reality value of most of them we cannot judge; just as they cannot be proved, neither can they be refuted ... scientific work is our only way to the knowledge of external reality." [61] In this same passage, he castigates those who retain the word "God" and give it some vague meaning. He likens religious teaching to the fairy tales we tell children, and though such stories may have some symbolic meaning, it is better to avoid "symbolic disguises" and to allow children to be told the truth suitable to their age of understanding. We must educate men to "reality" and the path to "reality" is through science. "Science is no illusion," he affirms, and "it would be an illusion to suppose that we could get anywhere else what it cannot give us." [62]

Here Freud shows his positivisitic hand, without qualification, and presents a totally secular view of man and nature. Furthermore, he so equates "reality" with "empirical fact" that he makes scientific methodology the exclusive approach to the real world. This is his faith! He is a believer! Interestingly enough, it is generally recognized that Freud was not an empiricist in the strict meaning of that term. He was really a philosophical psychologist who developed a theory of human nature based upon his limited clinical observations and physiological studies. It was not a theory that could be confirmed by public verification or defended on the grounds of statistical probability. Nonetheless, his view of man as an inwardly torn and alienated creature, who must learn to live with himself and his world as they exist, and not as one would like them to be, presents a "realistic" picture that is closely related to the themes of alienation in the existentialism of Sartre, Camus and others.

It is amazing to observe how so few people, who espouse many of Freud's ideas about man's nature, have read his writings. Yet the themes of "reaction formation" and "sublimation," as attempts to explain behavior, as well as the notion that religion is, in the final analysis, a "projection" of one's wishes into the nature of the universe in order to make life more bearable and tolerable, are widespread beliefs. As the result, morality and religion are viewed as subjective responses to real or imagined needs and so subjectivized that they are looked upon as having nothing to do with objective reality. Since their claims for truth can be neither affirmed nor denied by scientific or rational means, they are left in the limbo of environmentally-conditioned beliefs that may have emotional value but little or no cognitive value. Thus the claim that there is an objective moral order, or the belief that the word "God" has a referent outside of human consciousness, is "psychologized away," as a subjective belief, and has no place among men who know how such notions originate. Such beliefs can only be dealt with autobiographically and reflect only the disposition for belief of the individual who has not come of age.

The lack of interest in religion by the intellectual, in other than a phenomenological sense, is no happenstance. The scientific temper of our time has created a mentality that brackets out metaphysical and theological questions as unknowable; hence these subjects are interesting to the intellectual as he considers a wide variety of subjects, but they are not of pressing moment. If most men and women, who are faithful to their religious duties, believed that there was no source for their faith, but that worship was, in fact, talking to oneself, it is unlikely religion would be the pervasive power it is and has been in the lives of countless numbers of people. Even within the eastern religious tradition, where the line between the individual self and the One or the All is blurred, the self is nonetheless believed to have some ontological ground and root. When the religious and moral sentiments are identified with purely subjective meaning and are fit into a naturalistic and secular understanding, the death sentence for religion has been made, and the claims that a morality nurtured within a religious frame of reference becomes meaningless.

It should be kept in mind that Freud lived in a predominantly Roman Catholic environment and his attack was upon the religion of the masses. His correspondence with the Reverend Oskar Pfister,[63] an intelligent and informed Swiss Protestant minister, indicates that Freud was troubled by a man whose faith did not seem to be neurotically dependent-oriented. Freud's generalizations about the psychological roots of religion may be true in many cases, but unfortunately his main contacts were with religious people who were his patients. He failed to make explicit the fact that any relationship of dependence can become neurotic; but when he suggests that religion, by definition, breeds a potentially neurotic type of person he makes a generalization that cannot be substantiated in fact. Many people find in their faith an instrument for greater creativity, wholeness and freedom rather than increasing the neurotic tendency to fantasize or escape from reality.

Freud came from a nominally religious home; the family observed the Jewish holy days until the time of his father's death. His father revered the Scriptures and on Sigmund's thirty-fifth birthday presented him with the Phillippson version of the Bible, a German translation and commentary. As far as Freud's own household is concerned, his son reports that there was no trace of Jewish custom in the family; however, the family did celebrate Christmas and exchanged gifts by a candle-lit tree and gaily painted eggs at Eastertime, but neither practice had any religious significance. Throughout all of his adult life Freud was an avowed atheist and felt that religion was a harmful force in the life of man.[64] Nonetheless, the dominance of moral and religious questions in his writings indicates his interest in these kinds of problems. Whether it is due to his own inner struggle, or whether these issues were prompted by the dominance of their role in the lives of his patients, is difficult to answer.

As his major biographer Ernest Jones and others have pointed out, Freud was troubled, throughout his life, with the problem of death; perhaps this, in part, explains Freud's fascination with religious questions. Gregory Zillborg suggests that "the problem of religious faith in the broadest sense preoccupied Freud throughout his life." [65] Unfortunately Freud reduced religion to the "man in the street" variety. Zillborg [66] also points out that if such a reduction were applied to science, science would be seen as an art of making mechanical toys or building bridges and bulldozers. The fact is that theoretical science is a long way from popular conceptions of science in which the distinction between science and technology is blurred. Freud's inability to distinguish between religious faith that breeds neuroses and religious faith that makes men more self-fulfilled and whole, was due to his oversimplification of what religion is and misrepresents religion as only a psychological response to an instinctual or conditioned need.

NOTES

1. Francis Bacon, *The New Organon and Related Writings.* H. Anderson Fulton, Ed. (N.Y.: The Liberal Arts Press, 1960), p. 39.
2. *Ibid.,* XI, p. 43.
3. *Ibid.,* XXIII, p. 44.
4. *Ibid.,* XLI, p. 48.
5. *Ibid.,* LVI, p. 55.
6. *Ibid.,* LVIII, p. 56.
7. *Ibid.,* LXII, pp. 59, 60.
8. *Ibid.,* LXV, p. 62.
9. *Ibid.,* LXXXII, pp. 79, 80.
10. David Hume, *An Enquiry Concerning Human Understanding.* (Illinois: The Open Court Publishing Company, 1958), Section I, p. 8.
11. David Hume, *An Enquiry Concerning Human Understanding,* Section XII. *Philosophical works of David Hume,* Vol. 4. (Boston: Little, Brown and Company, 1854), pp. 187, 188.
12. Hume, *op. cit.,* p. 17.
13. W. Windelband, *A History of Philosophy.* (N.Y.: The Macmillan Co., 1919), p. 476.

14. David Hume, *An Inquiry Concerning the Principles of Morals,* Appendix I, *Philosophical Works, op. cit.,* Vol. IV, p. 357.
15. *Ibid.,* Section I, p. 236.
16. *Ibid.,* Section II, p. 243.
17. *Ibid.,* Section V, p. 295.
18. David Hume, *The Natural History of Religion, op. cit., Philosophical Works,* Vol. IV, p. 492.
19. David Hume, *Dialogues Concerning Natural Religion.* (N.Y.: Hafner Publishing Co., 1948). Henry Aiken, Ed., Part XII, p. 94.
20. *Ibid.,* pp. vii-xvii for Aiken's excellent introduction.
21. Hume, *op. cit., An Enquiry Concerning Human Understanding,* p. 67.
22. *Ibid.,* p. 81.
23. David Hume, *A Treatise of Human Nature.* (Illinois: Open Court Publishing Co., 1958), Part IV, Section VI, p. 258.
24. *Ibid.,* Part IV, Section VI, p. 260.
25. *Ibid.,* "Appendix," p. 275.
26. Auguste Comte, *Grands Types,* I., pp. 6, 7. As quoted by W. M. Simon, *European Positivism in the Nineteenth Century.* (Ithaca: Cornell University Press, 1963), p. 45.
27. Gertrud Lenzer, *Auguste Comte and Positivism: The Essential Writings,* Ed. (N.Y.: Harper Torchbooks, 1975), p. xliii.
28. *Ibid.,* p. 287.
29. Auguste Comte, *A General View of Positivism.* J.H. Bridges, Tr. (N.Y.: Robert Speller and Sons, 1957), p. 9. Official Centenary Edition of the International Auguste Comte Centenary Committee.
30. *Ibid.,* p. 26.
31. *Ibid.,* p. 34.
32. *Op. cit.,* Gertrud Lenzer, p. 72.

33. *Ibid.,* p. 83.
34. *Ibid.,* p. 261.
35. *Op. cit., A General View of Positivism,* p. 365.
36. *Ibid.,* p. 368.
37. *Ibid.,* p. 392.
38. *Ibid.,* p. 50.
39. Francis Darwin, Ed., *The Life and Letters of Charles Darwin.* (N.Y.: D. Appleton and Company, 1899), Vol. I, p. 41.
40. *Ibid.,* p. 51.
41. *Ibid.,* p. 75, 76.
42. Charles Darwin, *The Descent of Man.* (N.Y.: D. Appleton and Company, 1874), Second Edition, p. 1.
43. *Loc cit.*
44. *Ibid.,* p. 80.
45. *Ibid.,* pp. 127, 128.
46. *Ibid.,* pp. 128, 129.
47. *Ibid.,* p. 134.
48. Here I have relied primarily upon secondary sources: Philip Rieff, *Freud: The Mind of the Moralist.* (N.Y.: Viking Press, 1959); Clara Thompson, *Psychoanalysis: Evolution and Development.* (N.Y.: Grove Press, 1950; Clavin S. Hill, *A Primer of Freudian Psychology.* (N.Y.: A Mentor Book, 1954); Patrick Mulahy, *Oedipus, Myth and Complex.* (N.Y.: Grove Press, Inc., 1948).
49. *Sigmund Freud: Collected Papers* (James Strachey, Ed.) Vol. V, (London: The Hogarth Press, 1950) p. 135.
50. Philip Rieff, *op. cit.,* p. 59 as quoted from *The Ego and the Id,* p. 30.
51. Sigmund Freud, *Civilization and Its Discontents,* James Strachey, Ed. (N.Y: W. W. Norton Co., 1961), p. 47.
52. *Loc cit.*
53. *Ibid.,* p. 44.
54. *Ibid.,* p. 59.

55. Sigmund Freud, *The Future of an Illusion* W. D. Robson Scott, Tr. (N.Y.: Doubleday Anchor Books, 1957), p. 8.
56. *Civilization and Its Discontents, op. cit.,* p. 69.
57. *Ibid.,* pp. 70, 71.
58. *Ibid.,* p. 39.
59. *The Future of an Illusion, op. cit.,* p. 24.
60. Gregory Zillborg, *Psychoanalysis and Religion* (N.Y. Farrar, Straus and Cudahy, 1962), pp. 207, 208 as quoted from Ernest Jones, *The Life and Work of Sigmund Freud,* vol. 3, p. 368.
61. *The Future of an Illusion, op. cit.,* pp. 54, 55.
62. *Ibid.,* p. 102.
63. Ernst Freud and Heinrich Meng, Eds., *Psychoanalysis and Faith.* (N.Y.: Basic Books, Inc. 1963).
64. I am indebted to Reuben M. Rainey's *Freud as a Student of Religion: Perspectives on the Background and Development of His Thought.* (Missoula, Montana: Scholars Press, 1975) for this biographical data.
65. *Psychoanalysis and Religion, op. cit.,* 205.
66. Gregory Zillborg, *Freud and Religion* (Westminster, Md.: The Newman Press, 1958), p. 49.

Chapter III

The Religion of Secular Humanism Examined

A Parable

On an island cut off from intercourse with the outside world there lived a society of men who had once been devoted lovers of music but who in the course of generations, for reasons that do not concern us, gradually lost their hearing. Those music-loving ancestors had built temples in which it had long been the custom for the populace to assemble once a week and listen reverently to the ceremonial plucking of native instruments and the responsive singing of choir and congregation. They loved music to the point of worship and regarded it as a holy thing, the hearing and singing of which impressed itself as the most exalted form of human experience. Now when the populace became gradually stricken with deafness there was no

81

immediate change in their ceremonial habits. So solemn an institution and practice could not readily be abandoned. Conservatives still attended the Sabbath musical services because their fathers and mothers had done so; they went on plucking their harps and zithers and exercising their vocal cords even though the sounds became gradually dimmer to their perceptions and by the fourth or fifth generation were scarcely heard at all. At length the more inquisitive of these later descendants began to ask why the custom of plucking at strings while staring at hieroglyphic symbols and straining one's vocal chords to no purpose was ever originated, and why, having sprung from ancestral folly and superstition, it shouldn't be abandoned by men of a more enlightened age. Rebels began openly to denounce the hypocrisy of keeping up so meaningless a custom, and their arguments won many converts. Most men drifted into passive indifference. In time no one any longer attended the temple services except the priests and choirs whose prestige or livelihood depended upon doing so, the intellectually feeble who had no prop but custom, and a small remnant of men who still retained enough of the faculty of hearing to feel something of the ancient reverence for music. These last were dubbed mystics, and when noticed at all were made the butt of ridicule. Psychologists built ingenious theories to expose the causes of their delusion, while semanticists started a campaign to have words like *music, tone,* and *harmony* eliminated from common speech, on the ground that they were semantic blanks, mere vacant sounds without any referents in actual experience. Inasmuch as this peculiar society prided itself on being democratic and liberal, the music lovers were not prosecuted for heresy, but came to be tolerated as harmless old fogies who might serve usefully to illustrate the bigotry from which most of the citizenry had happily escaped. The whole thing was accepted as a clear proof of social and intellectual progress. And of course no one heeded or understood when once in a while a music lover, goaded into argument, would reply (in sign-language, presumably): 'It is not we who are deluded, but you, you, my friends, who are deaf!' [1]

Parables prove nothing, but they serve a useful purpose as a literary device to illustrate a fundamental insight or truth. There is little question that as man accepts a naturalistic world-view, his belief that the source of his moral and religious aspirations have an objective referent becomes less certain and finally fades into the limbo of subjectivity. As such, the problem of whether or not an objective referent exists in some theistic sense can be taken or left without jeopardizing a meaningful world-view. Theistic religious faith can be tucked away with other remnants of the past and the institutions built around these beliefs can be sustained by those who feel the need for them, but neither what they symbolically represent, nor what they might mean in the life of society bears any significant relationship to the future of man. When institutions die that were established to meet a human need, inevitably, other social forms arise attempting to fill the spiritual vacuum created by the absence of what has been rejected. It may be a Religion of Culture that stresses music and the arts, or it may be a Religion of the State, as in the case of the USSR, that attempts to fulfill these needs. History is replete with illustrations that "man cannot live by bread alone," and that he will usually identify with a social reality that expresses his hopes and aspirations in some ideal form. Such an inclination on the part of man may say something about him as a person and about the spiritual nature of the universe of which he is a part. But more about this later.

Religious Belief and the Positivistic Temper

I am using the term "positivistic" or "positivism" to denote a particular philosophical position that has become a dogma in British and American philosophy within the past forty years. It began with a group of European philosophers in the 1930's, known as the Viennese Circle, whose teachings spread to England and America in the form of "Logical Positivism," later called, "Logical Empiricism." I am fully aware that present day American and European "positivists" have moved beyond the positions of Moritz Schlick, A. J. Ayer, Rudolf Carnap and others and would like to be identified with linguistic-analytic philosophy. Nonetheless, some of the basic distinctions that A. J. Ayer made in his book, *Language, Truth and Logic,* are still important to understanding the development of the analytic movement. Ayer's influence is illustrated by a comment of one of my colleagues in philosophy regarding the writings of Paul Tillich when he said, "Paul Tillich's books are nonsense." To my mind, claims by analytic philosophers to the contrary, "logical positivism" is far from dead in its attack upon the very heart of the cognitive legitimacy of either theological or ethical statements.

Briefly stated, the distinction is made between cognitive and non-cognitive propositions. Cognitive or meaningful statements are of two types: (1) Analytic propositions that are tautological, or in the language of logic, the predicate adds nothing to the subject. For example, all triangles are comprised of three angles is a definition that cannot be refuted because the nature of triangularity is that of three angles. (2) Empirical or synthetic propositions that are *in principle* verifiable. That is, meaningful statements are those that are subject to verification by other observers; their truth or falsity is not a matter of speculation, but a question of "fact." Propositions are verifiable in "the strong sense" when the claim can be "conclusively established in experience," and it is verifiable "in the weak sense" if it is likely or probable.[2] Thus the criterion of verifiability becomes the means for certifying the "literal meaning" of an assertion. Many experiences may be emotionally significant, such as religious or ethical convictions, but these are essentially feeling states that reflect the attitude or preference of the individual who is making the religious or ethical utterance and have no "literal significance" whatever. As such, these statements are neither true nor false.

A number of years ago, Max Otto, Professor of Philosophy at the University of Wisconsin and well-known scientific humanist, came to our campus and began his lecture with this story. "Let us imagine," he said, "that I go into a service station and ask for a quart of oil for my car. The attendant brings a container of oil out to my automobile that looks like a pint. (This was in the old days when oil was dispensed from pouring cans that were filled from large barrels.) The longer I look at the oil can, the more convinced I am that it is a pint and not a quart. And so I ask the attendant to bring the oil can over to my car window and there, indelibly stamped on the outside of the container, are the words, 'One pint.' I point this out and then he says 'When I look at that can of oil, I am overcome with an emotion and intuition that assures me that it is a quart and not a pint! I don't care what it says on the label.' " And then Max Otto comes through with his punch line, "This is what we want to know—statements of fact that are verifiable and certain and not based upon intuition or subjective feeling."

This is obviously an inadequate analogy to the depth of religious, moral or aesthetic experience, but such a criterion for knowledge reflects the predominantly positivistic posture, in many philosophical circles, that have a profound bearing upon epistemological questions. Let us look at the implications of logical empiricism for what is "knowable":

(1) Metaphysical statements; (2) Religious claims for knowledge; (3) Ethical judgments.

First, metaphysical statements about ultimate reality or the nature of being "are nonsensical" [3] because they cannot be justified by the arbitrary definition of what constitutes factual, hence meaningful, assertions. The metaphysician who speaks of mind or ideas or forms as more real than the objects of sense experience is playing an intellectual game of words that has no literal meaning. Metaphysical problems, thus viewed, are "fictitious problems," in contrast to "genuine problems" that, in principle, have a way of being solved. Sidney Hook, humanist philosopher and one of the leaders of the humanistic movement, expresses concern over the renewed interest in metaphysics and ontology and the possibility of their "cognitive legitimacy" among such linguistic-analytic philosophers as Willard V. Quine, but more particularly in the philosophical writings of Heidegger, Hartmann, Tillich and others. His attack is upon the notion that ontological truths attempt to reveal the essential nature of Being *as such,* a knowledge about something that cannot be conveyed by the sciences. Hook argues that such a term as "Being" is indefinable and is only a word that cannot be demonstrated to exist in "reality." His conclusion, regarding either the cognitive or verbal legitimacy of the term, is devastating to anyone who might claim the ontological character of Being, when he says, "It is a word, that neither designates nor refers to anything observable or discernible in the world, and has neither a substantive nor attributive character." [4]

Likewise, Rudolf Carnap denies the cognitive meaningfulness of metaphysical statements by calling them "pseudo-statements," that is, from a point of view of logical analysis they *"are entirely meaningless,"*[5] from a strict interpretation of the meaning of that word. Since metaphysical statements are neither true nor false, there is no criterion, other than subjective, by which they can have meaning. If the metaphysician talks about the "principle" of "being" or of "existence," he is speaking of a reality that is not empirically observable. Carnap cites a number of similar terms that are meaningless: "the Absolute," "the Idea," "the Infinite," "objective spirit," "being-in-itself," "emanation," "the Ego,"—all in the verbal arsenal of the metaphysician. He concludes,

> The metaphysician tells us that empirical truth-conditions cannot be specified, if he adds that nevertheless he 'means' something, we know that this is merely an allusion to associate images and feelings, which however, do not bestow a meaning on the word. The alleged statements of metaphysics which contain such words have no sense, assert nothing, are mere pseudo-statements.[6]

Second, the implications of this view for religious statements are similar to metaphysical propositions because both types of language involve assertions about "realities" that are not confirmable through the ordinary use of empirical observation or confirmation. It is obvious that talk about God within a religious community has "meaning" in some contextual cognitive sense. More recent developments within the linguistic-analytic movement have included "God-talk" as at least contextually meaningful, but when the believer affirms the existence of God he means more than asserting a social concept as "real" and meaningful only to those who speak within a certain frame-of-reference of meaning. Furthermore, a religious person believes that

87

either a psychological explanation based upon the fulfillment of a human need, or a sociological analysis based upon the "reality" of a social phenomena, or a linguistic interest in the "meaning of the meaning" of theological language, do not do justice to the problem of "God's Reality." He finds the positivistic attempt to classify ideas according to prescribed definitions as arbitrary and its reductionistic character as doing violence to the richness and fullness of his experience that prompts him to say, "God exists!" In fact, for many believers, the affirmation of God's reality is more compelling and "common sense" than the affirmation that the external world of sense experience exists. I recognize that this is incomprehensible to the person unconsciously wedded to empirical observation and confirmation as the criteria for knowledge, but nevertheless this is the opinion of countless men and women who wear "spiritual glasses" in their perception of Reality. Try and prove the *real* existence of the external world to a Hindu or Christian mystic. It is arbitrary to say that their experiences are merely subjective in nature and have no objective referent. Those who claim an objective Source or Reality for their experiences are sensing another manifestation of Reality than those who insist that objective reality is only that which can be empirically demonstrated.

In the final analysis, the positivist's own bottom line, namely, verifiability as a criterion of meaning, is itself unverifiable, and that by limiting cognitive propositions to either tautologies, empirical statements, or the syntax of language, he adopts a definition and method that is self-authenticating—a notion analytic philosophers find offensive when knowledge is affirmed on the grounds of other criteria than those which they accept. Ayer clearly argues that "the verification principle" is a definition, not an empirical statement of fact. At the same time he contends it is not an "arbitrary definition" but attempts to establish the conditions for the acceptance and understanding of "common-sense and scientific statements" about the world "in which we live and move and have our being." The problem is that when a philosophy that tries to be "scientific" and makes its definitions for what is "meaningful" a paradigm for all philosophy, it is overreaching itself and implicitly makes a normative claim that does not do justice to the wide variety of theoretical claims for knowledge that mark the history of religious and philosophical thought. *The answers one gets to a problem are no richer or more significant than the methodology employed in the attempt to resolve the problem.*

In 1949 A. J. Ayer and Father Frederick C. Copleston engaged in a debate that was recorded by the British Broadcasting Corporation. Copleston's reply to Ayer regarding the "verification principle" is pertinent to our comments.

If you [Ayer] say that my factual statement, in order to be meaningful, must be verifiable, and if you mean, by verifiable, verifiable by sense experience, then surely you are presupposing that all reality is given in sense experience. If you are presupposing this, you are presupposing that there can be no such thing as metaphysical reality, and if you presuppose this you are presupposing a philosophical position which cannot be demonstrated by the principle of verification. It seems to me that logical positivism's claim to be what might call a neutral technique, whereas in reality it presupposes the truth of positivism ... it looks to me as though the principle of verifiability was cogitated partly in order to exclude metaphysical propositions from the range of meaningful propositions.[7]

As my colleague, Professor Dallas Willard points out, there is no way of proving the verifiability principle within the framework of positivistic concepts because statements about meaning cannot be verified by the senses. Meaning cannot be tasted, touched, smelled or seen. Criteria for meaning are intellectually posited categories that are established by the mind in dialogue with others through shared experiences.

The reason the debate with radical empiricism is so important for our discussion is due to the fact that an empirical bias, as science understands the term, undergirds, by and large, the attitudes of secular humanists toward theistic religion. They may not call religious claims to knowledge "nonsense," as in the case of the logical empiricist, but they do tend to look upon religious faith that is centered in an Object of faith as "fantasy," or "fiction," or "illusory," because the belief in the reality of God is not based on the hard data of empirical evidence. From this point of view, the secular or the "natural" is made Ultimate and is expressed in daily life as a functional type of atheism, though intellectually it may be argued that the posture is that of agnosticism. Functionally or operationally we act as though there *were* or *were not* a Divine Presence that either permeates the whole of nature, or is greater-than-nature. It is interesting that approximately ninety percent of the people of the United States are intellectual "believers," that is, they affirm the existence of a supernatural power they call "God," but have been so secularized by a materialistic society that they are functional atheists *except when some felt need* for religious faith arises. At the same time, probably a majority of the members of the academic community consider themselves intellectual agnostics, yet function as atheists. For most of them, religion is a part of the culture for which there is no deep feeling or commitment, one way or the other.

Most of us reflect the ambiguity of our society regarding religious questions, and consistency is not the virtue that best describes our lives. It is at this point that the secular, or naturalistically oriented person often finds humanism a source for commitment and faith that becomes his religion. As a result, the secular humanist functions as though the aspirations, goals and ideals of men were Ultimate and thus gives to his commitment a functional-ontological ground, though intellectually he may remain an agnostic regarding the ontological question on the theoretical level. Parenthetically, I might add if God is the Source of all good aspirations that improve the human lot on this planet and is the Source of all concerns for human justice and freedom enabling man to realize the full potential of what it means to be created in the "image of God," then the true atheist is the person who only cares for the plight of his fellows to the extent that his lack of concern for their well-being might affect his own happiness. This is what I meant by the comment that the committed secular humanist lives by a theoretical view of what mankind might become that has an implicit ontological ground.

The third aspect of logical empiricism's impact upon conventional forms of belief, that also relates to the subjective or relativistic view of naturalistic humanism, is the problem of ethics.[8] Traditionally, ethics has been defined as a discipline within philosophy that is concerned with the problem of what constitutes obligation or duty and the nature of the good. In contrast to a descriptive approach to these questions, ethics has stressed the prescriptive nature of normative judgments about good and bad, right and wrong. The history of ethical theory is replete with a variety of ethical theories ranging from the formalism of Kant's categorical imperative, as an a priori principle, to Mill's utilitarianism. With an increasing interest in empirical approaches to all questions, descriptive accounts of what men value, in contrast to what they ought to value, have dominated the social scientific scene. It is argued that there is no way to establish a universal ethic because men differ in the values they prefer; hence a phenomenological, or descriptive approach to ethical questions is mandated. Thus, through a study of cultures, life-styles and social patterns of value, the justification for these differing value-attitudes can be seen. Ayer's distinction between the cognitive and non-cognitive or emotive statements applies here. If I say, "Theft is wrong!" in some judgmental or normative sense, I am reflecting my displeasure with the act of stealing. Thus ethical statements are hortatory exclamations that indicate my emotional like or dislike for some particular type of attitude or behavior. Putting it in the jargon of sociology or psychology, ethical statements and attitudes are formulated by cultural influences that vary from time to time and from society to society. As in the case of the classic debate between Socrates and the Sophists, morality is rooted in *physis* or Nature (and here Socrates, through Plato, was speaking in the metaphysical sense), and not through *nomos* or convention. In the *Protagoras,* Plato suggests that the axioms for good or right are grounded in a trans-cultural reality that exists beyond the relativity of societies and men. There is little question that ethical relativism prevails within our society and that morals and ethics are the result of an environmentally-conditioned process, but that does not preclude the possibility that values have some ontological ground as well.

Most naturalistic humanists would call themselves ethical relativists, but when it comes to being counted on when principles of civil rights and human justice are involved, often their moral stance belies the relativism which they intellectually hold. I have observed this repeatedly among men and women who argue that all values are relative to place and time; yet will take moral stands, at great personal risk, because they believe the rights they are defending have more than passing value. I do not know that the philosophical views of the American Civil Liberties Union members has ever been determined, but I would imagine that most of the members of that organization would consider themselves moral relativists intellectually. Yet, the absolutism of their moral convictions about human rights is most impressive as they defend the rights of individuals, no matter what their political persuasion might be. Leaders of this organization act as though their views had some Ultimate value and typify, what I have called, an implicit "functional-ontological" approach to value questions. This is why so many people who find a grounding for their moral convictions in theistic religion have joined hands with human rights movements regardless of the social or political philosophy that might prompt the concern. The news pictures of the Selma, Alabama, civil rights march were an inspiration; men and women of a wide variety of creeds, philosophies, races, and social commitments joined hands and marched together because their cause was Right! For them, the moral stand they were taking was not merely a matter of convention or socially determined prejudice, it was an act that was True and Right and Good. The commitments of *Humanist Manifesto II* clearly indicate the social convictions that provide a convictional frame of reference for living. Paul A. Schilpp states it well when he says, "Ethical Religion is *commitment* to the highest, noblest, sublimest and best that I can think, imagine, or understand. And: it is *a way of life* commensurate with the greatness of that to which I have committed myself." [9]

Nonetheless, the frame of reference for secular humanism regarding what can be known remains within scientific and logical parameters. In the Preface of *The Humanist Alternative,* Paul Kurtz says concerning humanism's perspective on the world, "Using the powerful critical tools of science and logical analysis, modern man now recognizes that the universe has no special human meaning or purpose and that man is not a special product of creation. Anthropocentrism has at last been laid to rest." [10]

Belief Not Knowledge

We have defined secularism as a naturalistic, non-theistic understanding of the world of man's experience that precludes viewing the world in mentalistic or spiritual terms. Simply stated, the physical world as it appears to us within the space-time continuum constitutes objective reality and to suggest that there may be a "beyond" or that the universe is expressive of another realm of meaning and value that is grounded in a Reality beyond our immediate perceptions is an unnecessary and overly speculative hypothesis that cannot be verified through the commonly accepted procedures of observation and validation. Such a worldview is essentially a belief, or if you will, a type of faith that views all of reality from a certain perspective and adopts a methodology for confirming and exploring the implications of that belief-system. Claim for levels of knowing that begin from other premises or fit within some other belief-system are either looked upon with grave suspicion or denied as being worthy of investigation. Some years ago, after a class discussion on the problem of what constitutes the essential nature of man's being—what historically has been called the self, or the soul, or the psyche—I met, by happenstance, a colleague in psychology. I mentioned to him that we had been discussing a problem that really belonged in his field of inquiry; he passed off my comment by the observation, "Yes, that is an interesting question, but we do not *as yet* have the tools to investigate it." In other words, the problem was a pseudo-problem, hardly worth discussing. Curiously enough these are the kinds of questions my students want to discuss. Probably the reason my students are still asking these questions is because they have an intuitive sense of identity with men of all times and ages who have pondered these same questions and find the attempt to abort such questions, or place all questions worth asking within a quantitative or definitional frame of reference, too sterile and limiting. It is no happenstance that one of the strong reactions of the counter-culture of the 1960's was to the spiritual emptiness and irrelevance of many intellectual approaches to human problems because they somehow did not relate to the depth of human experience the students felt and experienced within themselves.

At the heart of the problem is the epistemological question—how do we know anything at all? The untutored in more advanced realms of scientific theory often assume that what we perceive somehow bears within itself its own meaning, forgetting that what makes the world intelligible is the conceptual structure we create to give our perceived world meaning. These conceptual frames of reference, or theories about the nature of the physical world, are modified as new evidence challenges old hypotheses, but essentially they are built upon the premise that there is a real world *out there* that we are observing and that the world we experience is not totally a projection of our own inner world of experience. What appears on the surface to be a "pure empiricism" is not so "pure" after examination. Data are gathered, sorted, classified and related to a cognitive configuration that gives the information meaning. But the general classification of the "relevance" of certain data and the "irrelevance" of other data are determined by the breadth of the experience of the observer and the way he thinks. This is the reason that in medicine, which is both an art and a science, certification for specialization is preceded by four to six years of residency under the tutelage of a master teacher who, by virtue of his experience, knowledge and skills, can help the student give conceptual meaning to

X-rays, laboratory reports, physical examinations of the patient, etc. He uses a technical vocabulary and many other symbolic means to teach his craft. The many and unexpected variables in each case make his task challenging because he can never know enough to deal with every situation. This principle not only applies to medicine but to all fields that are dealing with complex problems. Unfortunately, in an attempt to put a conceptual handle on a problem we often identify too quickly with a "school of thought" without adequate examination of the basic presuppositions upon which a particular approach to a problem is predicated. As "schools of thought" become fashionable and self-authenticating, they become entrenched within a tradition that borders on orthodoxy, a problem not unique to our religious tradition.

On the simplest level of experience, a baby is confronted with undifferentiated stimuli that have no meaning, other than some mass "out there" that simply exists. Such stimuli have a compelling impact upon the consciousness and only as his senses are sharpened and he is taught, for example, that certain colors have a name or certain other stimuli can be particularized and given meaning in some specific way, can he relate in self-conscious ways to his environment. In all probability he will consciously discover his own body first and then extend his conscious awareness to other areas of his experience.

Thus, through observation and through the ability of the mind to make connections between our separate experiences, we develop configurations of meaning and extrapolate from our experiences those aspects that can be brought into some orderly and uniform frame of reference. The unique power of the human mind arranges our experience, provoked by what Hume called the "internal" and "external" sense, and thus provides a basis for functioning in the world. Kant attempted to escape Hume's theoretical solipsism by ascribing to the mind certain "categories," or ways and forms of apprehension that were in some way a part of the nature of the knowing mind. For example, he posited that the reason for making "causal connections" between events is because the mind is so ordered that it constructs experience into some causal pattern. Whether or not "causality" exists "out there" is an open question; Kant remained skeptical about knowing anything "as it is," because the reflective process is once removed from the immediacy of the experience itself. Kant found the rationale for the religious view of life to be imbedded in moral experience and not in the realm of sense experience. He rejected the rationalistic basis of the ontological argument and found the teleological argument for God's existence the most plausible, but not convincing.

The point I am making is that both the epistemology of science and religion is grounded in certain beliefs about man and nature as well as in the relationship between the perceiver and the perceived. The claims that science and religion make for "knowledge" are subject to doubt and further inquiry, though the same empirical criteria for the claim, from the scientific frame of reference, are by necessity different from the criteria for "religious knowledge" that rests upon another realm and kind of meaning. In both realms, at best we only have psychological certitude and not certainty. Within the terms of science, we have probability and a degree of practical certainty; within the language of religion we have psychological certitude based upon the assumption that the universal outreach of the human spirit to the "beyond," as expressed in the religious traditions of mankind, is not wishful thinking, but reflects a universal quest for meaning beyond the immediacy of the present to the eternal.

The persistency of the religious question does not prove its objective reality; but it may be an indication that man is a part of a greater universe of meaning that many traditions call the One, or the All, or the Tao or God.

In a previously published paper,[11] I have argued that scientific statements and theological statements are related to configurations of meaning and that both theoretical science and theology are legitimate intellectual attempts to "make sense" out of our experience, though the source of the two types of experience may be in part separate and also overlap. The difference between the adequacy of the two views of reality lies within the world-view of the individual. Hence the belief-system colors what are viable cognitive options and what are not. For example, two geologists may look at the Grand Canyon with all of its majestic hue of colors and shades and one of them may say, "My god!"—an exclamation that reveals his response of aesthetic wonder and beauty, while the other geologist may say, "My God!" thus placing his experience within a theistic world-view that relates the sense of awe and wonder of the experience to God, as the Source of Beauty. In one sense, both geologists view the same Grand Canyon, but in another sense they see two different spectacles because their observations are filtered through their own frames of reference for meaning. As F. R. Tennant has so aptly stated, "What comes into—i.e. before—the mind, depends to some extent on the mind's tension; so that the mind is comparable to a slit in an elastic pouch, rather than to a slot in an iron automatic weighing machine."[12]

Henry Margenau points out that in trying to make the activities of the physical world intelligible it is difficult to distinguish that which is "immediately given" from the process of relating what is perceived to a frame of "orderly knowledge."[13] Also, Margenau's distinction between the "P-plane" of perceptions, the immediate data confronting consciousness, and the "C-field," behind it concepts or constructs which may or may not be related by direct correspondence to our perceptions, is an illuminating insight.[14] He further points out that the relationship between the mental construct and the percept is not self-evident or obvious because the configuration of meaning that helps integrate our perceptions emerges gradually through the slow process of applying the standards of coherence and consistency to the structure we create. "Our experience," he says, "confronts us with a P-plane which in its complete lack of organization and coherence defies our understanding. To alleviate our bafflement we set up correspondence between these factual experiences and certain constructs." [15] Margenau goes on to suggest that there may be a parallel between the relationship of percept to concept in the field of religion as well as physics; thus, "religion, too, can claim its due." [16]

However, the data of a religious understanding of Reality goes beyond that of the physical sciences, though it may include many observed aspects of the physical order. When theologians or philosophers of religion try to "prove" their case by appealing to the physical world and attempt to apply scientific methods of verification for the truth-value of their claim, they inevitably contribute to the age old conflict between science and religion. In my judgment, there is an inevitable conflict between the "truths" of science and the "truths" of religion when religionists affirm as "fact" that which seemingly contradicts the laws of nature.

A. D. White's volume on *The History of the Warfare between Science and Religion* is replete with illustrations of men and women who, in the name of religion, contradicted the evidence of scientific investigation on the grounds of tradition and religious authority. In the 16th century, Martin Luther criticized the Copernican heliocentric cosmology on the argument that Sacred Scripture teaches that Joshua made the sun to stand still and not the earth, the implication being that the sun is in motion around the earth. The

Darwin-Creationist debate still rages in certain parts of our own country; unfortunately, the science vs. religion issue is not dead. Biblical literalists, who defend the Biblical account as "factual" and remove these accounts from their historical and contextual pre-scientific settings, contribute to the estrangement of those who view "fact" as that which is verifiable. Another reason for the conflict between science and religion is due to some religionist's claim for absolute truth. Science, at its best, thinks in terms of hypotheses, probabilities and open systems; thus, when religious thinkers speak of absolute truths they not only forget a part of their own religious tradition that affirms "we see through a glass darkly," but also sidestep the interpretive element that enters into all claims for knowledge. I have tried to show, in this chapter, that all knowledge fits within a larger belief-system and in that sense, all beliefs are relative to that configuration of meaning. At the same time, I have suggested that this epistemological limitation on *certain* knowledge does not preclude the possibility of a reality that is greater than that of the space-time, physical universe of which we are a part. I have further suggested that at best we have psychological certitude regarding our affirmations, whether they be either scientific in nature or religious in nature, and that because of our finitude and limitations—cultural, temporal and personal—we can never have certainty.

The danger of comparing the types of certitude within the realms of religion and science is to assume that we can apply the same criteria for certitude to both. Religious claims for certitude are not predicated upon statistical probability because the range of referential experience is qualitatively different than that of translating the experience into quantitative terms. For example, it is true that when a Tibetan monk meditates his respiratory activities are altered to the extent that he practically has a flat EEG.

This is interesting information, but tells us very little about the *reality* of the experience he is having and can in no way indicate the ontological significance of the lived-through event. In other words, the facts of his posture, breathing, state of no-mind consciousness can be described, but all of these elements have little or no significance for the experiential certitude about the world and the self that such an activity provides. Paul Tillich rightly points out, "Almost all of the struggles between faith and knowledge are rooted in the wrong understanding of faith as a type of knowledge which has a low degree of evidence but is supported by religious authority." [17]

It is important to distinguish between belief and faith—a confusion that often leads to insoluble problems. In its earlier usage, 'belief' was commonly called 'faith,' but by the 14th century, especially in theological language, the word 'faith' superseded the term 'belief' and 'belief' came to mean primarily intellectual assent, a usage that is common to this day. 'Faith' refers to trust and confidence and fidelity. Unfortunately, we do not have a verb 'to faith' but must translate the word into 'to believe.' In both Greek and Latin there is a verbal form of the noun 'faith' enabling the unique meaning of the word to be put into verbal usage. It is quite different to say, "I believe in you," meaning I have no good reason to doubt your integrity, than it is to say, "I have *faith* in you," which raises the statement to a more inclusive level of response than mere intellectual assent. Perhaps the following distinctions will be useful regarding the 'belief' and 'faith' levels of response for both scientific statements and religious statements.

(1) *Belief as credulity.* The credulous person too quickly accepts another person's statements as true, either because of his supposed authority, or because of some charismatic quality the person might have. This is what Erich Fromm calls "irrational authority." In such cases, the individual

may be intimidated by the authority, or for a wide variety of reasons, accepts the word of the authority without further investigation. Beliefs are accepted and affirmed uncritically and on face value. In a day when so much knowledge has been discovered in almost every field of inquiry, it is impossible to investigate personally everything that is said; hence we rely to a large extent upon experts who have been certified by some peer group, only to discover that they are fallible and prone to error like everyone else. At best we hope that what is offered as responsible information is from what Socrates called, "a learned ignorance," and not from stupidity. For the most part, people are more greatly influenced by propaganda-motivated information than by scholarly reflection and a great deal of what we intellectually affirm is the result of the most recent "authority" we have read or whom we have heard speak. One of the primary purposes of education is to assist the move from the accepting and uncritical stage of belief to the critical and reflective level.

(2) *Belief as an intellectual postulate.* This involves a philosophical enterprise of making sense out of our experience and is related to the comment we have made previously about the necessity to provide meaningful frames of reference for experience through the development of configurations of meaning. The implications for scientific investigation are clear and have been alluded to many times in this essay. Within the realm of religious belief, humanistic or theistic, certain affirmations are made about the nature of man, his relationship to his fellows and his relationship to the cosmos that are postulated as "true," and thus provide a heuristic, or informative, value to the life-stance we may take. These theoretical positions inform and give substance to our behavior in contrast to a willy-nilly posture that responds irrationally to each situation as it arises. For example, if we say, there is a spiritual force in the universe

termed God, the affirmation is a postulate based upon certain interpretations of experience that makes-more-sense to affirm than to deny. Such a statement does not prove God's reality, but it does place the affirmation within a responsible intellectual frame of reference that fits into a consistent world-view and relates to everything else we think we have learned from our experiences. A number of years ago I was lecturing at a neighboring university and during the question period a member of the audience asked me, "You seem to believe in a spiritual reality within the universe, but I am sure you know that many of your colleagues, who are just as smart or maybe smarter than you are, either deny God's existence, or have no need to affirm His reality one way or the other. How do you explain this difference between your own beliefs and those of your respected colleagues?" I could only answer, "If my colleagues had read the same books I have read, had all of the experiences I have lived through, and intuitively and intellectually perceived my world as I understand it, they too would make the same postulational affirmation."

We are now moving from appearance to reality—an existential dimension that leads me to my third distinction.

(3) *Belief that becomes faith.* When a belief captures the imagination and prompts commitment and action consistent with that belief it becomes faith. At one time, "faculty psychology" was in vogue that viewed the human personality as consisting of emotions, will and intellect. Since that time, an organic understanding of human personality has been suggested as a more adequate model, due to the dynamic interrelatedness of how persons think and feel and do. Nonetheless, these distinctions are helpful in differentiating the various aspects of the ways we respond to persons and things. When we respond emotionally we are usually not very reflective and appear irrational. When we defend a position we take rationally, we call upon the resources of

the mind and intellect to our cause. And when we act upon what we believe, we make a decision and choice that involves our wills. Now faith includes all of these elements: emotions, will and intellect. In other words, it is the whole person responding. The dedication that men and women give to what they *believe in,* for whatever reason, is an act of *faithing* and is an admixture of all three aspects of the personality. If one *faiths,* he is no longer an observer, he is a participant. The distinction between *belief about* and *faith in* applies to the difference between intellectual assent to a proposition and the *experience of* something that warrants commitment and trust.

Faith does not eliminate either intellectual or existential doubt. As Tillich has pointed out repeatedly in his writings, faith and doubt lie within each other. As long as we are bound by the limitations of finitude, we can never be sure that the object of our faith warrants the existential truth-claim we may make for its objective reality. At the same time, faith expresses itself within a space-time order and is not removed from ordinary experience. This is why the artificial bifurcation of the secular and the divine, or the profane and the holy is often arbitrary, because in the faith-response we are never sure what is objectively out-there. In a sense the subject-object dichotomy has been obliterated and it is only after reflection that we make the separation. Faith, as an existential response involving the whole person, functions within a continuum of meaning. As Zen teachings stress, man *faiths* within an organic context of meaning that defies the artificial distinctions we reflectively and self-consciously make in our analysis of experience. Nonetheless, responsible responses require such analysis and are fruitful if we recognize that the process of analysis may lead to a paralysis of spirit that destroys the meaning of faith rather than enriches its value. Whether or not this occurs depends in large part upon the predisposition of the analyzer; the paralysis of analysis need not be the outcome. This is why a posture of *reverent skepticism* is appropriate to the life of faith. It may not avoid the snares of credulous faith, but it will help purify faith by the contributions that scholarship, learning and knowledge bring to faith. Also, such a posture contributes to the positive value of self-criticism within the religious community that tends to rely on self-authenticating truth that is beyond criticism.

Summarizing what I have tried to say, a faith-response involves the whole person responding to an object that he deems worthy of his devotion. If it is blind, it becomes victimized by credulity, and if it is only intellectually grounded it lacks the emotional quality that will motivate the will to act. Thus, faith as a kind of knowledge, is in part an inferential judgment though it bears within itself the primacy of a *lived through* event. It is the force and strength and compelling character of its immediacy that prompts the faith-response. It is unlikely that one would respond with his total self unless that to which he was responding bore within itself some feature that was difficult to resist. We have suggested that faith gives to the experient psychological certitude, not certainty. *If we had certainty, there would be no need for faith.* While science is concerned primarily with demonstrative certitude (empirical verification), the search for meaning in our lives lies within the realm of psychological certitude (faith). The truth that is confirmed through the life of faith can be affirmed in the spirit of openness and tentativity as we seek new interpretations and deeper insights concerning what faith means and implies. However, as Gordon Kaufman points out, the final ground of all our thinking about faith is a kind of "ultimate religious pragmatism in which we decide in faith to attempt to live by our faith ... Verification here is 'experiential' rather than 'experimental': it proceeds within the life process itself rather than through isolation of a segment of the life process which is then studied externally." [18]

This leads us to an examination of the complexity of the problem of the nature of meaning—its ambiguity and referential character.

Meaning and the Language of Faith

As the line between percept and concept is blurred, so is the distinction unclear between the affective and cognitive aspects of our experience. Our need for a rational or intellectual self-image prompts us to separate the cognitive from the emotive, but in the actual living of life, this is very difficult to do, though definitionally we can make the distinction. We use the term, 'meaning,' broadly in common parlance, and our statement that "it was a meaningful experience," may range in reference from a friendship to a philosophical discussion. Obviously, the former experience involves primarily affective responses while the latter is more cognitive in nature. In any event, we use the same term to describe different types of experience. or we may say that "it was a *deeply* meaningful experience;" here again there is an admixture of both intellectual and emotional factors reflected by the statement. Usually we use the term in a positive way, though at times we may refer to some tragic experience as providing a special kind of meaning for our lives. A great deal has been written about the "meaninglessness" of modern existence, that contemporary man has lost his sense of direction and that the impersonal nature of a technologically-oriented society has dehumanized him so that he feels as though he were a cog in a wheel of fate over which he has no control. In this context, to find meaning for one's life is to discover a sense of destiny and purpose that enables the individual to rise

106

above, or transcend the deterministic aspects of his environment. Here the term "meaning" is used in more of an existential and personal sense in contrast to a consciously cognitive or intellectual activity that would attempt to build a system of meaning, and thus provide a coherent philosophy of life, though such activity might be involved, to a lesser or greater degree, depending on the disposition, background and interests of the individual.

If the term 'meaning' is restricted to "meaningful statements," then one by definition limits meaningful discourse to a cognitive enterprise that consists of tautologies or empirically verifiable propositions. This is not to suggest that we should not be as clear as possible in stating what we mean, but often the depth of our experience may have ineffable qualities that defy adequate verbal expression. Definitions are attempts to give precision of meaning to that to which they refer. When we say, "I think I understand what you mean" we are asking for more specificity, either by a more careful use of words or possibly by analogy or simile. In addition, our statement may have some connotative meaning or implication besides what is primarily denoted. Since the meaning of words is socially and culturally influenced, it is difficult to convey the intended meaning of a word if one is trying to converse with a person from another culture. Also, within the same culture, a term may have a pejorative meaning for one person and a positive meaning for another. For example, the noun "heretic" might have a negative connotation for a conservatively-oriented individual while the same word might have a favorable meaning for a liberal. If one understood the word from its Latin source, it means, "able to choose." Attempts to give definitional meaning to the words we use are difficult because of the dialectical relationship between the definition and the person who places the definition within his own context of meaning. I suppose the reason why logic and mathematics are so attractive is because their validity is predicated upon their own internal consistency. I am aware of the significant work in linguistic analysis done within the last twenty-five years that has sensitized us to the use of words and the problems of ambiguity. This area of scholarship, though limited, has had a profound influence on those interested in the responsible use of religious language.[19]

Meaning is not only conveyed through words, but through many different ways of expression. Gestures and other forms of body-language reveal levels of meaning that often belie what is said. The rhetoric of the words may mean one thing, but the way it is said often conveys something quite different. Or the facial expression, tone of voice and the like may reinforce verbal forms of meaning that are more powerful in their effect than the choice of words themselves. Thus oral communication is broader than mere syntax; it involves a set of complex relationships between the speaker and the hearer.

Because faith-responses to reality involve the dynamic interrelationship of all phases of the personality, meaning is more adequately expressed through symbol, myth and allegory in contrast to statements that have literal significance or meaning. For example, when we experience love, we are prone to convey its meaning through poetry and the language of imagery in contrast to empirical statements of fact. Or when we find meaning in a poem or work of art, we relate to the object in both an analytic and non-analytic way. We may compare it with other poems we have read or other paintings we have seen, but there is also the non-rational response that perceives and intuits the meaning it has for us as we stand in its presence, as it were. In fact, the empirical data regarding the artistic creation may be quite irrelevant to its intended and real meaning. The factual information regarding who painted it, when it was painted, the schools of thought that influenced the painter, the pigment of the paint that was used are secondarily relevant to the lived-through meaning of the painting as it reflects something about an aspect of reality we have not felt or understood before. Thus the intermingling of feeling and understanding, two words used in the previous sentence, are naturally linked in the experience itself. We make the distinction post-experientially upon reflection. The separation of the two aspects of experience are academic and interesting but not vital to what is experienced. The same observations could be made about a wide variety of literary and artistic forms of expression that have had meaning for men and women in all places and times. We have been speaking of the arts but the same may be said of science though it may not be so obvious. If the transmission of scientific knowledge were totally effable, there would be no need for laboratory classes.

In short, the language of religion seems to be more akin to the language of the arts than it is to science; the language of faith is the language of symbols, myths, allegories, rites and ceremonies. Peter Munz distinguishes between the symbol picture of reality—that is the religious understanding—and the positive scientific picture of the world.

Thus the language of religion primarily consists of myths and symbols that provide us "ordinary knowledge of a somewhat extraordinary picture." [20] From this view, the religious picture of the world does not rival the scientific view, but complements it and views it from another perspective. Let us examine the role of myth and symbol as the language of faith.

(1) *The role of myth.* Unfortunately, the word "myth" is identified with a story that is untrue and equated with a fable or falsehood. This is particularly true in those religious circles that defend the truth-value of their tradition on the grounds that it is based upon historical fact and not on myth or even legend. It is helpful to distinguish between

109

legend and myth: Legend is based upon a nucleus of probable historical fact that has been embellished over the years. For example, there is enough historical evidence to support the claim that there was a man by the name of Abraham that figured large in the history of the Jewish people, but to suggest that all of the accounts of his activities are historically true borders on credulity. By and large, Abraham's life and adventures are based upon an oral tradition that preceded the written record by hundreds of years. This, and many other factors, make it difficult to defend the literal account as written, not to mention Sarah's pregnancy at age ninety.

In contrast, myth is centered in an idea or problem that is a part of a tradition and is told in story form. History is full of such accounts that have been retained within the tradition even after the people have become more sophisticated in their views. Why is this so? Probably because these myths convey a depth and richness of meaning that cannot be transferred from one generation to the next in a better way. In the foreword note of Andrew Greeley's book, *The Jesus Myth,* he says, "The word 'myth' is used in the title of this volume in a specific and definite sense. A myth is a symbolic story which demonstrates, in Alan Watts' words, 'the inner meaning of the universe and of human life.' To say that Jesus is a myth is not to say that he is a legend but that his life and message are an attempt to demonstrate [this] 'meaning'." [21] Here the noted and controversial Roman Catholic writer uses the term in a most positive sense and attempts to place the richness of the Christian tradition within a larger than literal frame of reference of meaning.

Historically, ancient myths performed a unifying and integrative function by relating man, the cosmos and the sacred. For example in the story of Moses receiving the tablets on Mt. Sinai, the sacred and the profane are united in an account that reveals or uncovers the fundamental Jewish conviction of God's relationship to His people. The Story of the Fall makes vivid man's estrangement from himself and reality—an existential truth that can be best told in the form of a story. As developed in the history of a people, myth as sacred story finds expression through ritual as sacred event. One of the reasons that sacramental rites persist, in spite of all efforts to desacralize them through "exposing" their "mythological" character, is because they speak directly to the human condition and have an ontic character (i.e. reveal an essential truth) that defies destruction. To suggest that such activities are mere remnants of the primitive within man is to do injustice to their symbolic significance in the life of a people.

The Story of Christmas is a beautiful illustration of the mythic-ontic power of sacred story. In spite of all of the historical and gynecological problems it might present, the story lives on because it describes the possibilities of hope and faith and love as these values are expressed in a simple account of a baby born in a manger. And so we place a crèche in our homes and listen to the carols that speak to our inner sense of what constitutes the good life for man and, as the result, our lives are ennobled and enriched. A myth, among other things, is a symbolic story; it may deal with tragedy or ecstasy, but it attempts to disclose meanings for us that might otherwise be overlooked. In many cases there is the union of the mythological-historical-existential elements. That is to say, the sacred story is cast within a particular setting and time in history but its meaning and significance become an existential reality for the teller of the story. But it does not end there. Its existential character continues with the tradition and is relived by succeeding generations of people who enter into its spirit.

In my judgment, despite the criticisms that have been made of his views, Rudolf Bultmann [22] has made a distinct contribution to an understanding of myth within the Christian tradition. He urges us to "demythologize" many of the Biblical accounts that are viewed literally because they seem incredible to post-Copernican man. Thus beliefs in demons and spirits, or in heaven and hell, or the language of the creeds and sacraments that speak of invisible essences as existing within material objects such as bread and wine, are incomprehensible to the scientific mind. At the same time, these stories and symbols, expressed in mythological form, bear an insight and truth that are worthy of penetration. Within them is a *message* about man and his existence that is concerned with the great issues of life: death, evil, suffering, redemption, hope, justice, love, etc. The problem for modern man is to get behind the myth to its intended meaning and then relate that understanding to his own life. If he literalizes the myth he is apt to stop one step short of discovering its real meaning because he is prone to justify the historical accuracy of the story and fail to penetrate the *message* it bears. I attended Sunday School all of my childhood and inevitably the teacher would try to prove that the story of Jonah and the great fish was literally possible because of an account of a fisherman in the 19th century who fell overboard, somewhere in the Mediterranean, and was "swallowed" by a large fish and survived to tell his story. Triumphantly, the teacher would then tell us, "You see, boys and girls, the story of Jonah is true." Not until I got to graduate school did I learn that one of the insights of the story is that God loves and cares for an individual though he may try to run away from Him.

The truth of a myth, like a work of art, resides in its "power to evoke in us an experience which we hold to be genuine." [23] Mythological forms that deal with man's origin, destiny, hopes, fears and intuitions about himself in relationship to others and his universe, provide richer sources for meaning "than is the image of the barren atomic topography to which the ideal of detached observations seeks to reduce these matters." [24] It is interesting that when we read a story, or see a painting, or hear a great musical composition we often say, "It speaks to me," as though it were some *real* "entity" that carries within itself a message for us. What we see, or hear, or read may not even be a product of our own culture; yet, it may bear within itself a *quality* that is relative to the society and person who gave it first expression, and at the same time bear a trans-cultural character that approaches a universality of appeal. Our intellectual and analytic life is overly prone to place experience within an either/or frame of reference. We identify it as either subjective in nature, or we plead for its basic objective character. We have already seen how artificial and arbitrary this distinction is in the dynamic interface between the perceiver and the perceived in the variety of meanings man gives to his perceptions. This same observation holds true of the role that myths play in our discovery of hidden meanings that are not obvious on the surface level of sense experience. If one admits that existential reality is a kind of reality that is neither totally subjective nor totally objective, one can begin to grasp the levels of meaning and reality which religious language attempts to reveal. As many writers point out, science itself has gone beyond the "myth" or "model" of a Newtonian mechanistic view of nature to a different model that insists upon the relativity of our description of how the universe functions as well as the complex and organic structure of reality.

Earl R. MacCormac points out that most philosophers of science today recognize that all theoretical terms used in scientific discourse cannot be reduced to observational terms. He further suggests that both scientific and theological attempts to express what reality is, or might be, resort to metaphorical and mythological language.[25] At best, all forms of human expression that seek to reveal the *real*, are limited to fallible ways for conveying meaning, whether it be through myth, allegory, parable, metaphor or the symbolic portrayals of the arts. We need to be open to all of these avenues of expression as we attempt to understand the mystery and depth of a reality that escapes encapsulation in any one form.[26]

(2) *The role of symbol.* A symbol stands for or denotes something other than itself, not by an exact replication or resemblance but in some general or even vague way. For example, the signet of a magistrate may appear on a coin of the realm, symbolic of the power of the ruler, or the seal of the President of the United States may be placed on a podium where he is speaking to symbolize his authority and place in the life of the nation. The meaning of symbols are not self-evident—they must be related to other aspects of experience that give them significance and force.

Paul Tillich makes a helpful distinction between a sign and a symbol.[27] A sign points to an object in which there is a one-to-one relationship between itself and its referent. For example, a red light at an intersection means stop and there is no ambiguity about it. A picture of a skull and cross bones on a bottle means poison without question. Signs stand for what they represent and nothing more; by and large they are uninteresting and serve little imaginative purpose. One glance gives us all the information we need in responding to what it means. Signs have an agreed-upon meaning which serve practical and useful functions in the daily commerce of life. Their "literal significance" enables us to conduct ourselves in some orderly fashion with some expectation that other persons will live by a similar understanding of what the signs mean. Thus, the mathematical "symbols" are, in this sense, "signs." Letters, numbers and to a certain extent words, if carefully defined with an agreed-upon meaning and usage, perform this function.

In contrast, symbols are quite different. They represent a

richness and depth of meaning that excites the imagination because the relationship between the symbol and its referent is ambiguous and unclear. Symbols provide the means for expressing feeling states and convictions that are believed to be of significance and importance. They are not mere propositions with an identifiable subject and predicate that can be logically analyzed and separated; instead, they reflect an interface for expressing the interrelatedness of the cognitive and affective aspects of our experience, though they cannot be reduced to either without doing an injustice to their unique function and nature. They bear an existential meaning that distinguishes their function from pure conceptualization. In this sense, symbols are very much like myths because they unveil structures of reality and bring meaning into human existence by providing what Mircea Eliade calls, "existential revelations for the man who deciphers their message." [28]

As applied to the language of faith, symbols provide a primary medium for expressing that which is beyond expression. Take, for example, the attempt on the part of the great religions of the world to express infinity: The All, the Tao, the Absolute, the One or the more familiar term, God. Eastern religions are more ready to leave these terms undefined, and perhaps appropriately so, because they are beyond definition, while we in the West have a compunction for definition in our attempt to be clear. But even after our efforts to communicate what is meant by theological terms, we are left with a symbol that escapes our full comprehension. In my judgment, Tillich's insight is most helpful when he says, "Religiously speaking, God transcends his own name." [29] Tillich further suggests that in this notion of God there are two elements: (1) The immediacy of an experience that is ultimate and not symbolic in itself; and (2) an "element of concreteness" that is experienced in the ordinary affairs of life and symbolically applied to God.[30]

For example, those experiences that have some intrinsic value and are viewed by many people as "sacred" or "holy" or "divine" because they speak of infinity and bear within themselves a quality of ultimacy that find their most adequate verbal expression by the use of such terms.

The primacy of the experience men have called "religious" has been well-nigh universal, and has included the Holy or the Sacred or the Other. Rudolf Otto, in his classic work, *The Idea of the Holy,* speaks of the sense of the *numinous* (the holy) as the *mysterium tremendum,* a "presence of that which is a *Mystery* inexpressible and above all creatures," evoking within man a sense of "awe." [31] The sense of the *numinous* is non-rational, a "mental state [that] is perfectly *sui generis* and irreducible to any other; and therefore, like every absolutely primary and elementary datum, while it admits of being discussed, it cannot be strictly defined." [32] If this be true of the datum of religious awareness, then all attempts to give conceptual meaning to the experience is on a secondary level of reflecting about that which has been immediately felt. I have suggested earlier that religious forms of expression are more akin to poetry than to almost any other media for expressing our deepest responses. Otto gives examples of the "numinous" in poetry, hymn and liturgy covering a wide range of expressions in Hindu writings.[33] These poetic expressions attempt to express the uniqueness of religious experience and the object of that experience. Wilbur Urban comments on Otto's expressions of the numinous, through poetry, by pointing out that the poet "catches something about both nature and man which the scientist misses," he further adds that "there is such a thing as poetic truth and that poetry, as symbolic form, expresses an aspect of nature, both human and physical, which cannot be expressed in any other way." [34] The primacy and universality of the religious response, thus described, proves nothing about the nature of reality, but it may provide a clue and ground for a religious realism that affirms the reality of a Referent people throughout the ages have called by a wide variety of names. There is little question that the attributes of that Referent are seen in the relative terms of various cultural symbols. When any group sets its symbolic forms in concrete, as it were, and literalizes them, they become signs and are seen as truth itself! When the forms expressing the divine are understood as symbols only, pointing to a Reality that is greater than the symbol itself, men will learn to be tolerant of each other's religious traditions and will realize that each unique form and symbol complements each other in the human attempt to comprehend, at least in part, the mystery of the divine. Perhaps Philip Wheelright's word of caution is appropriate as we conclude this section of this chapter, "If reality is largely fluid and half-paradoxical, steel nets are not the best instruments for taking samples of it." [35]

Secular Humanism's Limited World-View

Leo Rosten spent several afternoons with Bertrand Russell a number of years ago and among other issues they discussed religion. Russell maintained a consistent skepticism regarding God's existence, but toward the end of the discussion Rosten inquired,

'Let us suppose, sir, that after you have left this sorry vale, you actually found yourself in heaven, standing before the Throne. There, in all his glory, sat the Lord—not Lord Russell, sir: God.' Russell winced. 'What would you think?'
'I would think I was dreaming.'

'But suppose you realized you were not? Suppose that there, before your very eyes, beyond a shadow of a doubt, was God. What would you say?'

The pixie wrinkled his nose. 'I probably would ask, Sir, why did you not give me better evidence?' [36]

It would be interesting to know what kind and how much evidence Bertrand Russell would demand in order to be convinced. Since he stands within the scientific-naturalistic tradition, I would assume that it would have to be the type of evidence that would warrant a reasonable postulate similar to scientific theories about the physical world. There is little question in my mind that an important element in the religious response to reality is the "will to believe," and that such a disposition is equally true of any other response we might make to what we conceive reality to be. To deny that the subjective element does not enter the criteria for reasonableness in scientific enquiry is to oversimplify the complexity of the epistemological process. As we have noted previously, two equally competent natural scientists can work in the same laboratory or view the same heavens and one find "evidence" for the existence of an "ultra-natural" dimension of reality, while the other sees no supporting evidence for such a claim.

As William James pointed out, it is only when the religious question becomes more than a casual option that the viability of belief really has force and moment in our lives. He calls this a "genuine option." Such choices for belief and action are both intellectual and "passional decisions"— the latter probably playing more of a role than the former, if the decision for or against belief is pressing and is believed to make a difference, particularly if the affirmation or denial has some truth-value.[37] The same element of passional belief enters into moral judgments and attitudes as well. I agree with James when he says, "Moral scepticism

118

can no more be refuted or proved by logic than intellectual scepticism can. When we stick to it that there is truth (be it of either kind), we do so with our whole nature, and resolve to stand or fall by the results. The sceptic with his whole nature adopts the doubting attitude; but which of us is the wiser, Omniscience only knows." [38] I am not willing to stand on James' instrumental or pragmatic theory of truth, but I am suggesting that his introduction of an existential element into the religious and moral questions of life is relevant to an adequate understanding of the rationale we give for belief or disbelief. I would not want to make an entire case for the relationship of psychological factors to the world-view one might hold, but some writers [39] have suggested that there may be a correlation between an individual's sense of alienation to others and his world and his religious views. That is to say, the possibility of an element of psychological projection might be a factor in an atheist's world-view in which he has 'read' the universe in terms of his own experience. This is twisting the Freudian thesis, that religion is essentially a process of psychological projection to compensate for one's own weakness, to the notion that an atheistic world-view might equally be a projection. Though the observation may be relevant to the causes of belief and disbelief, it reduces the issue to a matter of psychological or social conditioning—factors that are relevant—but not all-encompassing. This is the issue. Social-psychological-biological determinists want it their way only. It is when we take half-truths, and make them whole truths, that a dogmatism emerges that seeks validation for its own theory.

In spite of what I have just stated, it is my contention that if reasonability be understood as an attempt to make sense out of our experience, then the nonrational as well as the rational aspects of our lives must be viewed as a part of what constitutes a meaningful world-view. The scientific-

119

naturalistic posture is not primarily interested in "what it all means" because such a concern is so vast and comprehensive one cannot fit every experience into a meaningful whole. As difficult as this task might be—and philosophers have spent years and written volumes to achieve this goal of a unified philosophical perspective—it seems to me that this is the philosophical challenge that is precluded by the essentially encapsulating method of scientific investigation. Let me be more specific.

Sidney Hook links the scientific approach to reality with naturalism in an unequivocal way. For example, he suggests, "naturalistic humanism . . . holds that the occurrence of *all* (italics mine) qualities and events depends upon the organization of a material system in space-time, and that their emergence, development and disappearance are determined by change in such organization." [40] Furthermore, "Insofar as our age requires a unifying faith, it is clear that it cannot be found in any official doctrine or creed but rather in the commitment to the processes and methods of critical intelligence." [41] A more direct relationship between naturalism and science is stated when he says, "what is involved in the scientific method of inquiry is what we mean by naturalism, and the characteristic doctrine of naturalism like the denial of disembodied spirits generalize the cumulative evidence won by the use of this method." And finally, he describes the scientific method as fundamental to the naturalistic posture: "What all naturalists agree on is 'the irreducibility' of a certain method by which new knowledge is achieved and tested." [42]

My objections here are to the all-inclusive character of and faith in the scientific method; theological and metaphysical claims to truth are bracketed out because they cannot be judged or tested by a method that has been chosen to investigate what is true or real. As it pertains to a belief in God, the argument would go something like this:

Since the existence of God can be neither empirically demonstrated nor falsified, the problem cannot be resolved. Furthermore, if God is defined as a 'spirit,' there is no way to observe God's activities and if it is argued that the effects of God's activities are observable in nature, there is no way to measure this activity and trace it to its original source. To make the term God equivalent to the notion of 'atom,' 'velocity,' or 'energy' is not justified, because we can measure the effects of these 'constructs' and thus justify them as legitimate concepts. Furthermore, the theoretical constructs of science serve the practical purposes of predicting how nature will function and provide the basis for our modern technology that builds bridges and places men on the moon. Thus, there must be some correspondence between our 'theories' and the nature of the universe, though we can never be sure of the adequacy of our theories as new discoveries emerge. Finally, to suggest that we push beyond the theories that enable us to carry on our scientific work to some more ultimate structure of reality, may be intellectually provocative, but not basic to our enterprise. To ask the question concerning what is the meaning of the ultimate nature of reality is to ask an unanswerable question.

As one of my colleagues in experimental psychology said in a discussion not long ago when we were pressing such questions as the nature of man, reality, the good life and such, "Leave us alone to do our work! These kinds of questions have no relevance to our inquiry." But I would argue that they have a great deal of relevance, not only because the investigation of anything whatever is a human enterprise, but also because every investigator has a hidden philosophical agenda regarding the method and nature of his inquiry that affect, either directly or indirectly, his investigations.

Not only is the naturalistic world-view limited by the predominant influence of the scientific method for investigating what "is," but in addition the scientific method is predicated upon a certain view of the universe that may say something about the nature of the universe itself, though the assumptions are not claimed to be an affirmation. I refer specifically to the assumption that the universe is intelligible, that is, it can be rationally understood, at least in part; that it functions in fairly predictable ways; that it is more unified than disunified; and the human inquiry concerning how it functions is a necessary and worthwhile enterprise. That is to say there may be a reason why there is some correlation and even correspondence between our mental constructs and what is "out there." These assumptions implicit within the scientific method are more dependent upon the medieval world-view that attributed the order and dependability of nature to a belief in God, as the symbol for order, than most naturalists recognize. Lynn D. White rightly points out that the monotheistic world-view, in contrast to the pagan notion of capricious deities, prepared the soil for the intellectual viability of a rational and scientific approach to nature's secrets. He says, "As the triumphant chant, 'I believe in one God, the Father Almighty,' rang through the new churches of the northern frontier, another foundation stone of the modern world was laid, the concept of an orderly and intelligible universe." [43]

It is what is implied by a scientific model of the universe that is of special import for an adequate metaphysical view of reality. The functional "as if" principle, upon which the scientific method is predicated, bespeaks a continuity of nature that links it into one great ecosystem that bears within itself a kind of "meaning" that man attempts to understand. This image of nature differs from viewing the universe as a collocation of entities that fortuitously have arranged themselves in ways that man *somehow* makes intelligible by relating their parts into purely artificial conceptual configurations in order to make sense out of them as they function without direction or purpose. Siegfried Müller-Markus points out that logical and mathematical theories do correspond to what is "real," but even after our analysis of the structure of a theory, we are still left with the problem of *why* such theories say something about reality.[44] It seems to me that the tradition for the scientific mentality to put a ceiling on its world-view limits the possibilities for meaning. It is at this point the metaphysician makes a contribution by pointing out the possible implications for a more adequate world-view that may lie behind the assumptions that are functionally accepted in an almost a priori way.

Henry Margenau calls these practical presuppositions the "metaphysical principles of science," that are an important aspect of the scientist's search for those laws of nature that "supervene upon and regulate tentatively chosen constructs of explanation." [45] Some of these assumptions are: Cognitive constructs must be "multiply connected," that is, they must bear a relationship of internal consistency and unity with other aspects of the construct system. Another principle is causality, not seen from either an Aristotelian or Newtonian understanding, but as "a relation between constructs" and as a "relation between *states,* or conditions of physical systems,"[46] By "states" he means "a set of observables" that helps describe and explain the nature of the system. In addition, the scientist seeks a "formal elegance" for his theory that is closely aligned with principles of simplicity and symmetry. Simply stated, the most desirable theory is one in which there is the least degree of variance in its application. As I have already stated, there is the assumption that a correspondence between a theory of reality and the nature of reality is possible. We will refer again to the issue of nature's intelligibility in the last chapter when we deal with the heuristic value of a theistic model of the universe.

Closely related to this problem is that of reductionism. As scientists break reality down into more minute parts and as the degree of specialization increases with the knowledge explosion that is, at times, staggering, the tendency is to forget that the one aspect of reality under scrutiny has been lifted out of the natural habitat of its organic relationship to that from which it has been separated. This is particularly true in dealing with the problem of "life," "force," or "energy" that is not observed directly, but inferred from what is perceived. We have earlier commented on the "nothing but" fallacy that often occurs when one observes that there is a correlation between one event and another—the temptation is to make a correlative relationship one of identity. For example, the mind-body problem is not dead and there are still those in the neuro-psychological field that take the problem of "mind" seriously. Sir John Eccles' and Roger W. Sperry's reflective writings on this problem are well known.[47] Long ago Plato commented on the type of reductionism that identifies thought, will and moral action with some material reality as absurd and superficial because the distinction is not made "between the cause of a thing, and the conditions without which it could not be a cause."[48] Plato did not deny, in regard to moral judgment, that his ability to do what he thought was right was related to his bodily functions, but he added, "to say that it is because of them that I do what I am doing, and not through choice of what is best—although my actions are controlled by Mind—would be a very lax and inaccurate form of expression."[49] He was affirming the philosophical principle that correlation is not identity. It is not my intention to get into the mind-body problem, only to suggest that the tendency of naturalistic reductionism to view mind or spirit as purely epiphenomenal is an over-simplification.

Henri Bergson reacted negatively to a type of reductionism that reduces the whole to its parts. He pointed out that when reality is segmented and parts are removed from their context, a necessary method in scientific investigation, the bit or piece of reality is no longer what it was in its vital relationship to the continuum from which it was separated. He argued for the necessary role of intuition that could perceive, as it were, through the eye of the mind, the interconnectedness of reality. It is this perception that gives reality a different dimension of meaning and viability. Bergson was not anti-scientific. Rather, he was insisting upon the very limited view of reality science could give due to its circumscribed methodology that in turn affected what it could, in principle, perceive. He further postulated the reality of an *elan vital* that provided an explanation for the vitality of the organic wholeness of nature.

The problems created when so called "natural reality" is reduced to some "material" substratum, not only apply to understanding the world of nature, but also relate to aesthetic, moral and religious experience. By and large, secular humanists accept the claims for the validity of these experiences as subjective and interpretive responses to types of experience that are identified by these names. We call an experience religious, moral or aesthetic because we have been conditioned to equate certain subjective experiences with referents that produce the stimuli so identified. When such an interpretation of these types of responses is made, the ontological significance of the experience is disregarded and is viewed from a psycho-social perspective. I suggest this is a type of reductionism that is inevitable when secular humanists attempt to understand or analyze such experiences in terms of a method that is inadequate to the nature of the experience. The contribution of the phenomenological movement, beginning with Husserl and later expressed in the existentialism of Merleau-Ponty, Marcel, Buber and others, is the idea that within human experience, whether it be of persons or things, there is an encounter of subject and object, or being and being, that gives that experience significance and meaning. From this point of view, ontology is not reduced to psychology, but the reality of being is experienced within our own space-time world of existence. Due to the anti-metaphysical bias and common sense predisposition of a naturalistic interpretation of all experience, the depth of the encounter within the dialogic situation is often overlooked. The experience of other conscious selves and our experience with nature evoke within us a sense of the "moral," and the "beautiful," that defies reduction to the categories of understanding that scientific naturalism imposes. The same applies to religious experience that is grounded in a sense of the "numinous" that, according to Otto, is as much a "given" within reality as any other datum. When secular humanists state that these experiences are accepted for their pragmatic value in the enrichment of human life and that any attempt to fit them into some larger ontological configuration of meaning is a fruitless, speculative, intellectual endeavor that has no value for the merit of the experience, it seems to me that a limit has been imposed on one's world-view that contradicts the attempt on the part of countless numbers of reflective persons to relate these profoundly significant experiences to a realm of being that in some sense transcends our commonsense notions of reality.

What Abraham Maslow calls "peak experiences" may be an inkling of another dimension of meaning that transcends the experient. Maslow does not pursue the ontological implications of these experiences in terms of a world-view that would include a Divine Spirit or God, because he is wedded to a need-fulfillment orientation to behavior. Thus he neither accepts nor rejects the ontologically-transcendent source for high moments in life that illuminate consciousness and raise it to a new level of awareness.[50] This tendency on the part of the humanistic movement in psychology to sidestep the metaphysical question is in part due, I think, to the fact that the leaders of Third Force psychology, as it is often called, want to be "empirical" and "scientific" and not alienate their equally biased colleagues who are philosophical naturalists. This comment is based upon an extensive reading of the literature in the field and upon brief conversations with Rollo May, Charlotte Buhler and J.F.T. Bugental as well as limited correspondence with the late Abraham Maslow. This charge may be less true of May who couches his metaphysical position in psychological language that is fraught with many of Paul Tillich's ideas about the nature of being.

It may be that man's persistent thrust towards self-transcendence is due to the nature of his own being that is grounded in a greater realm of Being than that of the space-time world. This also might be called the outreach of the human spirit that refuses to be encapsulated within the arbitary boundaries of any dogma or doctrine about what reality is. This may be the real meaning of the human spirit that can soar beyond the confines of the spatial and temporal world to regions that most men have not discovered. Plato's Allegory of the Cave illustrates how most men are chained to the world of sense, or in the language of our times, how they are wed to a methodology that limits their perception of what is most real. The seer, the mystic, the reflective and meditative man seeks to break these chains that can stifle the human spirit as much as any political or religious external authority. Within our own time, perhaps the meaning of the "freedom of the spirit" should be seen in this light. The problem is to place the non-rational aspects of our experience within some rationally responsible frame of reference that at the same time does not stifle or destroy that which is originally experienced. Otto saw this clearly when he pointed out that the sense of the "holy" involves component elements that are both rational and non-rational. Though the sense of the numinous may be realized through the sensory and empirical world, it does not arise out of them—a distinction Kant made regarding the relationship between the faculty of cognition and the senses. In my view, the compelling and inexplicable character of moral and aesthetic experience is likewise a part of the "data" of human experience that a naturalistic range of vision cannot place within a realm of being that does justice to their deservedly ontological character.

I have tried to show that when naturalism is wedded to a scientific investigation of what is real, it provides a truncated view of reality that does not place our deeper understanding of nature and man within an adequate conceptual frame of reference of meaning. The issue centers in what conceptual world-view provides an adequate ontological ground for the richness and depth of our experience. One cannot be dogmatic about this issue. It is indeed a personal question, but this does not mean that it is unimportant.

There is a tendency today to downgrade the significance of ideological issues—particularly in a democratic society that prides itself in being tolerant and open-minded. But often tolerance is a mask for indifference and anti-intellectualism. I believe that historical analysis will vindicate the view that the ideological struggles throughout time have made a difference concerning the type of lives we lead and our destiny as human beings. Though I would argue strenuously that the methods of scientific investigation are not applicable to many of the issues we are discussing, the spirit of science, which insists upon openness to new insights and the value of honest inquiry, is a basic principle that should temper all attempts to arrive at answers. This principle, combined with the Socratic emphasis upon humility, should mark all attempts to penetrate the mysteries of our existence.

The Illusion of Secular Humanism?

The title of this section of the chapter is in the form of a question. As the Vedas teach, all may be *maya* or illusion; man's capacity for deceiving and being deceived is great. We trust our senses only to realize that we have been in error; we depend upon consensual validation later to discover that majority opinion can also be wrong. For hundreds of years man believed that the sun revolved around the earth; he could see it rise in the east and set in the west. The confirmation was validated by the senses—after all anyone can see that it crosses the heavens. Now we know it was not true and the heliocentric view of the earth's relationship to the sun is established beyond reasonable doubt. Rationalists of the 17th and 18th centuries believed in self-evident truths that were beyond question and could be recognized by any rational agent. And so runs the story of the history of human thought. Therefore, to declare dogmatically that either a non-theistic or theistic view of the universe is a true picture of reality is to make an affirmation that may or may not be true. At the same time, our minds reach out for answers to questions that science cannot deal with—they are persistent questions that emerge out of the human mind's insatiable curiosity about all facets of experience. The child's impertinent question *why*, which he manages to suppress when he discovers it is too threatening for most adults, haunts us all in the moment of our deepest reflection. Though we may not be explicit in the answer we give to this question, we opt for either a functional life-style that will bring us some degree of peace of mind and fulfillment, or we may turn to some belief system that provides a foundation for our lives. Man cannot live without some frames of reference or belief systems, which are expressed in the way he thinks and acts. Secular humanism arose as a reaction to the restrictive character of authoritarian systems of belief that were too narrow. There is little question that the spirit of freedom, prompted by humanistic movements, had a liberating influence upon the life of modern man; yet at the same time, man must make some affirmations about his life and the end toward which he will use his freedom. The problem is to be open to new experiences and knowledge as they might illuminate our understanding and retain a central focus to our lives that will provide enough emotional, psychological and intellectual stability for us to prevail in a world that is torn by dissension, strife and unrest. As I have suggested earlier, when we replace one frame of orientation to life for another, it is easy to substitute one dogmatism for another.

One of the current movements that has attracted a great many people, who have rejected traditional religion and a theistic life orientation, has been self-realization humanism. Erich Fromm's writings have probably been more widely read than any of the other leaders of the movement. His books cover a wide range of topics ranging from political and social issues to the most profound philosophical and theological questions. Though he says that the most important thing is for human beings to care for one another and that the theistic nontheistic issue is of secondary importance, he has supported clearly, in his writings, a naturalistic world-view as preferred to theistic belief.[51] For example, after discussing the existential dichotomies that beset every individual, he says,

There is only one solution to his problem: to face the truth, to acknowledge his fundamental aloneness and solitude in a universe indifferent to his fate, to recognize that there is no power transcending him which can solve his problems for him ... If he faces the truth without panic he will recognize that there is no meaning to life except the meaning man gives his life by the unfolding of his powers, by living productively; and that only constant vigilance, activity, and effort can keep us from failing in the one task that matters—the full development of our powers within the limitations set by the laws or our existence.[52]

How does Fromm know that "there is only one solution to his [man's] problem ... to recognize there is no power transcending him"? This is a statement in reaction to a radical supernaturalism that characterizes a large part of the theistic community, to be sure, but not all of it. Parenthetically, it is interesting to note that Fromm was an orthodox Jew until he was twenty-seven years of age and, in my judgment, many of his attitudes about religion reflect a reaction to orthodoxy. This is particularly true in his tendency to identify theistic religion with some form of "irrational authority," that intimidates the individual to believe rather than appealing to his rational capacities. This response to theistic religion is quite typical of many naturalistic humanists who are *reacting against* a dogmatic religious background, and, in the process, have thrown out the substantive aspects of a theistic world-view that provides a rationale for values they still cherish. This is also true, I think, within the secular Jewish humanistic community where there are strong ethnic ties for Jewish values and traditions, but a rejection of the religious underpinnings that are so closely interwoven into the tradition they cannot be neatly separated. The same problem holds true for many Christians, who have retained the humanistic values of their tradition but reject the theological frame of reference that gave rise to these values. I recognize that western values are a synthesis of Jewish/Greek/Roman/Christian cultural traditions, but the predominance of Jewish and Christian theological categories are most apparent within our own tradition. The emotional ties to the values these beliefs fostered are firm, but for many the rationale no longer makes sense; hence the conceptual structure is rejected and the values are retained. Often western humanistic history is interpreted as beginning with the Periclean age of Greece, then the jump is made to the Renaissance without reference to the periods before or after. The result is a kind of cultural plagiarism that does violence to the significant role that both Judaism and Christianity have played in shaping our lives and the humanistic tradition of which we are a part. The interface between the religious convictions of our Founding Fathers and democracy is well established; [53] yet, these historical facts are often glossed over as irrelevant to the American story. The reasons for this state of affairs is understandable as intolerance and bigotry characterized too much of our religious history, but the alternative of secularizing our sense of tradition can be equally harmful to the deepening of a sense of humanistic values within the lives of our young. The issue is not that of indoctrination versus no indoctrination; it is a question of fidelity to our tradition in all of its aspects—both negative and positive.

Returning to Fromm's dogmatic statement regarding man's aloneness in a universe indifferent to his fate, Fromm is reflecting the possible 'illusion' that man is capable of dealing with his problems and needs no spiritual sustenance that comes from some cosmic source some men have called God. Fromm's writings are filled with references to man's "spiritual" needs that transcend his physical needs. However, Fromm does not find any basis for postulating a metaphysical ground for the source or fulfillment of the needs he recognizes as universal. He even speaks of the "self" that must be fulfilled and identifies this with the core of personality, the source for creativity and freedom; yet, he will not attribute to the self metaphysical status. He refers more to Aristotle and Spinoza than any of the other philosophers and agrees with their notion that there are certain *given* potentialities within human nature that are crying out for fulfillment, but he feels no conceptual obligation to attribute these potentialities to either a metaphysical or theological principle rooted in human nature.[54] Fromm also stresses the importance and value of love and identifies a productive character orientation with both the ability to love and the power to think creatively. Here again he finds no need to attribute these potentialities to a metaphysical source, but accepts them as a *given* within human nature that needs no further explanation. I suggest that he and many others within the naturalistic humanistic movement, place a ceiling on their world-view and that their understanding of man is much richer than the conceptual framework upon which they rest. Their convictions are impregnated with the values and beliefs of a tradition that is rejected and it is unlikely that the humanism they represent would have been possible without the nurture of the religious movement that gave it force and momentum.

The fact of man's increasing interdependence is undeniable in a world where nations rely upon each other's natural resources. Humanists stress this interdependence and the need for, not only small communities where human values and growth can be shared and realized, but also for a world community that is bound by a mutual concern for all human beings that transcends local and national boundaries which tend to separate man from man. Man's dependence upon nature and natural forces over which he has limited control is also increasingly realized. As our ecological crisis intensifies, we begin to realize that unless we cooperate with nature's ways, human life may become extinct. On the other hand, as man advances in scientific and technological knowledge, it is very easy for him to be so impressed by his own achievements that he no longer recognizes he is a dependent creature and that the ultimate source for his existence lies beyond himself. Naturalistic humanists have no difficulty recognizing this danger; however, they do not view this as a cosmic dependence in any traditionally religious sense, and find no conceptual need to attribute the activities of nature to a Cosmic Source. I am reminded of the story of Job and his travails. At one point, he becomes so distressed that a righteous God would not vindicate him that he wants to curse God. Whereupon God asks Job some very haunting questions,

> Where were you when I laid the foundation of the earth? Have you commanded the morning since your days began, and caused the dawn to know its place? ... Is it by your wisdom that the hawk soars, and spreads his wings toward the south? Is it at your command that the eagle mounts up and makes his nest on high? [55]

The Book of Job is a curious admixture of humanistic elements, urging Job to quit complaining and take it like a man, on the one hand, and a stress upon the fact of Job's dependence upon the cosmic order within which and behind which there is Yahweh, on the other hand.

Strictly speaking man creates nothing, if creation is viewed as bringing into being something out of nothing. Man brings into new relationships what is already there, but he does not create out of a vacuum. The Protestant Reformers, as well as St. Augustine and others, were insistent upon the distinction between God as creator and man as creature. This emphasis was an attempt to help man recognize his appropriate place in the universal order of creation and not fall under the 'illusion' of independence and autonomy.

Historically this sense of dependence has been expressed through the symbolic expressions of worship through rites, ceremonies and liturgies. The secular humanist's view that worship of a power greater than oneself tends to be dehumanizing and increases a sense of helplessness, may or may not be true depending upon the attitude of the worshiper himself. Although any dependent relationship might take neurotic forms, there is nothing within a sense of dependence upon God, as expressed through forms of worship, that, in itself, weakens the personality. Seeking spiritual sustenance through meditation, prayer and praise may strengthen the individual to cope with the exigencies of life. Just as man receives nourishment for his body from the food he eats, and the ability to cope with the uncertainties of life from the friendships and close relationships he enjoys, so may man find spiritual subsistence from his relationship with the divine. Secular humanism's assumption that man's spiritual potential can be realized through intellectual, social and aesthetic forms of expression may be a type of wishful thinking that borders on the 'illusory.' In addition, the spiritual anxiety he experiences created by the dichotomies that are a part of his existence (e.g. life *and* death; personal identity *and* social identification; self-realization *and* the limitations of the space-time world) may be caused by his search for the infinite within the finite alone. St. Augustine's classic observation that "our souls are restless until they find their rest in Thee, O God," may be the fact of the matter.

Closely related to this problem is that of idolatry, that is, making certain values ultimate that are not worthy of ultimacy. If man is both finite and infinite, strictly temporal values will not satisfy the depth of the human spirit. Secular

135

self-realization humanists and Christian humanists agree that power, wealth, success, possessions and the like are inadequate to meet man's deepest needs; they are like a mirage on the desert. Also, they agree, as in the case of Erich Fromm and Paul Tillich, that the full life cannot be achieved unless the individual becomes a person within a community of persons.[56] This involves shared values and feelings and the experience of intersubjectivity that enhances the lives of those who experience it. Martin Buber, likewise, shares this conviction. The question is: Are such experiences enough? Will the shared values within the context of a community suffice? It is at this point that the theist breaks ranks with the secular humanist because such avenues for self-discovery lack the vertical dimension of meaning. As I shall suggest in the last chapter, such experiences may provide a clue to the meaning of divine love and the transcendent dimension of human experience, but they do not in and of themselves provide the full experience of the infinite that men seek.

For all practical purposes, the humanist's moral ideal becomes reified, and becomes worthy of a person's commitment and faith. Though conceptually it is not viewed as having ontological status, its practical function effects a change in values and life-styles. Thus the ideal value is defended on practical grounds and is acted upon "as if" it were true in some more ultimate sense. Due to the fact that naturalistic humanist movements have no rites, sacraments or liturgies deeply rooted within a tradition that symbolize their ontological source, the abstract nature of their appeal lacks the force that has characterized the religious traditions of mankind. The attempt to substitute a religion of culture, in its literary and artistic forms, for these traditions provides aesthetic and emotional satisfaction for many, but lacks explicit moral teachings that provide ethical guidelines for living. I grant that one might extrapolate a harmony and unity within human artistic creations that lift the spirit to seek a harmony and unity for one's own life. Or one might derive moral lessons from great plays and stories that portray the nature of human existence and the outreach of the human spirit, but such expressions appear in such a wide variety of forms that it becomes difficult to find a continuing thread of meaning that would give direction to human life unless one settled for one form of expression and made that the source of his inspiration and commitment.

I have already stated that there is a close tie between poetic and religious forms of expression, but I do not think that one can be a substitute for the other. If there be an eternal Referent which man seeks throughout his life that is more than a projection of man's highest aspirations, then it would appear that it would be greater than man and the natural order though it might be expressed within that order of being. Naturalistic humanists stress the creative arts and their value for man, but see them as a product of man's creation and leave the ontological question there. I am intrigued by the musician or the aesthete who can play or listen to Bach's great works and have no feeling or thought, one way or the other, about the conceptual or theological frame of reference that gave rise to this music.

The USSR cherishes its literary, artistic and musical tradition as well as the beauty of its churches which they are restoring in all of their ancient splendor.[57] However, in their attempt to thoroughly secularize the society through the education of the young and other means, the churches become Museums, along with the Hermitage Museum and Tretyikov Gallery, as expressions of the human spirit. But when the question is asked, "The outreach of the human spirit to what?" it seems to me that from a secular perspective there can be no satisfactory answer. Parenthetically, I might add that in my judgment any religious renewal that might appear in the Soviet Union in the future will come through the arts, because they cherish their cultural history which is closely linked with their religious tradition. As our own society becomes increasingly secularized, it seems to me that fitting the artistic, literary and musical expressions which were prompted by a religious perspective into a naturalistic terminus will be increasingly difficult to do. Since our society is neither totally secular nor religious, but a unique admixture of both, this is no immediate problem, but once the secular becomes a widely accepted doctrine about man and his experiences, concerted efforts will have to be made to separate the cultural expressions of that tradition from its historic roots, particularly if it is believed that they are harmful to the progress and future of the society. This is precisely the problem in the USSR, which is officially atheistic, but yet finds itself in the "embarrassing" position of having to place the cultural expressions of the past they cherish within their present philosophical posture.

Granted that all we know may be an illusion, but we can try to develop an understanding of human experience that will do justice to its depth and richness of meaning. It seems to me that the kind of faith which the naturalistic humanist places in man is unwarranted, not only in the light of the human propensity toward evil and destruction, but also because of the bipolarity of man's own nature, that is, the interrelationship between the finite and the infinite. Whatever the human spirit might be, it seems to be a well-nigh universal phenomenon that man seeks to transcend the limitations of space and time and that the spirit of man seeks renewal and nourishment from sources other than itself. The major religions of the world attempt to fulfill this need in a wide variety of ways. The 'illusion' of secular humanism may be the assumption that the irascibility of the human spirit that cries out for meaning in an absurd world is an unjustified and irrational protest that must be accepted. There is no easy answer to this outcry, but the clamor itself may be a clue that the hurt is justified and that the resolution lies in another direction than its acceptance. The tyranny of the Myth of Sisyphus plagues us all; there may be a better way for man than to accept the deterministic limitations of his plight. Naturalistic humanists themselves are divided on this point; nonetheless, whether the humanist accepts the circularity of absurdity, or the hope of a better future through science, reason and better social conditions in which to live, humanists agree that there is no Source that man can tap for the renewal of his spirit other than that within man himself. It seems to me that a humanism can be combined with a theistic world-view that provides a greater possibility for renewal than naturalism itself can proffer. I disagree with Paul Kurtz when he suggests a "Christian Humanism would be possible only for those who are willing to admit that they are atheistic Humanists." [58] We now turn to the meaning and implications of a theistic world-view.

NOTES

1. Philip Wheelwright, *A Critical Introduction to Ethics.* (New York: The Odyssey Press, 1949), pp. 398, 399. Used by permission.
2. A.J. Ayer, *Language, Truth and Logic.* (N.Y.: Dover Publications, 1946), pp. 36, 37.
3. *Ibid.,* p. 41.
4. Sidney Hook, *The Quest for Being.* (N.Y.: St. Martin's Press, 1961), p. 164. This is a detailed analysis of the problem of meaning of Being and should be studied by all serious students of the problem.
5. A. J. Ayer, Ed., *Logical Positivism.* (Glencoe: The Free Press, 1959). Rudolf Carnap, "The Elimination of Meta-

physics through Logical Analysis of Language," p. 61.

6. *Ibid.,* p. 67.

7. MacGregor-Robb, *Readings in Religious Philosophy.* (Boston: Houghton Mifflin Co., 1962). "Logical Positivism: Discussion between Professor Ayer and Father Copleston," p. 345.

8. Theodore T. Lafferty, *Nature and Values.* (Columbia: University of South Carolina Press, 1976), p. 13. As quoted from Ayer et al., *The Revolution in Philosophy,* p. 75. I found Lafferty's chapter, "Epistemological Preliminaries," particularly insightful as related to the limitations and overly simplistic nature of analytic attempts to deal with questions that do not fit the "analytic model."

9. Paul A. Schilpp, "Is Religious Humanism Enough?" *Religious Humanism,* Vol. VI, Number 4, Autumn, 1972, p. 148.

10. *Op cit., The Humanist Alternative,* p. 5.

11. J. Wesley Robb, "Science and Theology," *The Personalist,* Vol. 43, No. 1, Winter, 1962, pp. 57-69.

12. F. R. Tennant, *Philosophical Theology.* (Cambridge: The University Press, 1935), I, p. 222.

13. Henry Margenau, *The Nature of Physical Reality.* (N.Y.: McGraw-Hill Book Co., Inc., 1950), Chapters 1-5 are particularly insightful as related to the problem of the epistemology of science. Chapter 5 on the "Metaphysical Requirements on Constructs" provides a philosophical understanding of the assumptions upon which the scientific method is predicated.

14. Henry Margenau, "Truth in Science and Religion," in *Science Ponders Religion,* Ed. Harlow Shapley (New York: Appleton-Century-Crofts, 1960), pp. 102-105.

15. *Ibid.,* p. 106.

16. *Ibid.,* p. 115. Also, see his essay, "The Method of Sci-

ence and the Meaning of Reality," in *Integrative Principles of Modern Thought,* Ed., Henry Margenau, (N.Y.: Gordon and Breach, Science Publishers, 1972), pp. 3-43. Also, my article, "Faith Not Knowledge," *Religion in Life,* Winter 1964, 65 is related to this overall problem; the passages from Margenau and Tennant were referred to in that essay.

17. Paul Tillich, *Dynamics of Faith.* (N.Y.: Harper and Bros., 1957), p. 33.

18. Gordon Kaufman, *Relativism, Knowledge, and Faith.* (Chicago: The University of Chicago Press, 1906), pp. 115-116.

19. I refer to some of the scholars who have dealt in depth with the problem of religious language: Langdon Gilkey, Ian Ramsey, John Hutchison, Frederick Ferré, Stuart C. Brown, Edward Cell, Frank B. Dilley, John Macquarrie and W. Frazer Mitchell.

20. Peter Munz, *The Problem of Religious Knowledge.* (London: SCM Press, Ltd., 1959), p. 41.

21. Andrew M. Greeley, *The Jesus Myth.* (N.Y.: Doubleday and Company, 1971), p. 11.

22. Rudolf Bultmann, "The New Testament and Mythology," in Bartsch-Fuller, Ed. *Kerygma and Myth.* (London: SPCK, 1960), p. 16.

23. Michael Polanyi and Harry Prosch, *Meaning.* (Chicago: The University of Chicago Press, 1975), p. 146.

24. *Ibid.,* p. 147.

25. Earl R. MacCormac, *Metaphor and Myth in Science and Religion.* (Durham: Duke University Press, 1976). An excellent historical review of the use of myth and metaphor in the language of science and theology. However, he describes both religious and scientific myths as emerging from two sources: (1) When a hypothetical explanation becomes a literal description of

the way things are believed to be. (2) From the root-metaphor that underlies the language forms of each. (p. 128).

This view differs from other notions of archaic myth as portraying the immediacy of an experience of an individual or group which is deeply felt and for which special significance and meaning is made—what John MacQuarrie calls "that wholeness of feeling that is below the level of discursive thinking." *God-Talk*, (London: SCM Press, Ltd., 1967), p. 174. MacCormac's use of "myth" is nearer to a theoretical construct than a lived-through event in the way I have been using the term in this essay.

26. Joseph Royce, *The Encapsulated Man.* (N.Y.: D. Van Nostrand, Inc., 1964). A most fruitful discussion by a distinguished psychologist who deals with many of the themes of this chapter.

27. Paul Tillich, *Dynamics of Faith.* (N.Y.: Harper and Brothers, 1957), pp. 41ff.

28. Eliade and Kitagawa, Eds. *The History of Religions: Essays in Methodology.* (Chicago: University of Chicago Press, 1959), pp. 102, 103 as quoted in Thomas Altizer, "The Religious Meaning of Myth and Symbol" appearing in *Truth, Myth and Symbol,* Altizer et. al., Eds. (Englewood Cliffs: Prentice-Hall, 1962), p. 89. In the quotation Eliade is speaking primarily of the role and meaning of symbols.

29. Tillich, *op. cit.*, pp. 44, 45.

30. *Ibid.,* p. 46.

31. Rudolf Otto, *The Idea of the Holy.* (London: Oxford University Press, 1926). pp. 13, 14.

32. *Ibid.,* p. 7.

33. *Ibid.,* Appendix II, pp. 191 ff.

34. Wilbur M. Urban, *Language and Reality.* (London: George Allen and Unwin Ltd., 1939), p. 578.

35. Philip Wheelwright, *Metaphor and Reality*. (Bloomington: Indiana University Press, 1962), p. 128.
36. Leo Rosten, "Bertrand Russell and God: A Memoir." *Saturday Review*/World, 2/23/74, p. 26.
37. William James, *Essays in Pragmatism*. "The Will to Believe." Alburey Castell, Ed., (N.Y.: Hafner Publishing Co., 1949), p. 95.
38. *Ibid.*, pp. 103, 104.
39. See Patrick Masterson, *Atheism and Alienation*. (Notre Dame: Univ. of Notre Dame Press, 1971), and Luijpen-Koren. *Religion and Atheism*, (Pittsburgh: Duquesne University Press, 1971). Both of these volumes deal with the philosophical roots of atheism.
40. Sidney Hook, *The Quest for Being*. (N.Y.: St. Martin's Press, 1961), p. 202.
41. *Ibid.*, p. 207.
42. *Ibid.*, pp. 173, 174, 191.
43. Lynn D. White, "The Significance of Medieval Christianity." George F. Thomas, Ed., *The Vitality of the Christian Tradition*. (London: Harper and Brothers, 1945), pp. 96, 97.
44. Margenau, *op. cit.*, *Integrative Principles of Modern Thought*. Article by Sigfried Müller-Markus, "Science and Faith," p. 504.
45. *Ibid.*, "The Method of Science and the Meaning of Reality," p. 26.
46. Margenau, *op. cit.*, *The Nature of Physical Reality*, p. 95. Some of the metaphysical assumptions of science are treated here and in the essay referred to above.
47. Two essays in particular are relevant: Sir John Eccles, *The Brain and the Person*. The Boyer Lectures, 1965, Australian Broadcasting Commission. Roger W. Sperry, "Mind, Brain and Humanist Values," appearing in *New Views of the Nature of Man*. John R. Platt, Ed. (Chicago: Univ. of Chicago Press, 1965). Also, Eric

P. Polten, *Critique of the Psycho-Physical Identity Theory.* (Paris: Mouton and Co., 1973).

48. Plato, *Phaedo,* Hugh Tredennick, Tr., in *The Last Days of Socrates.* (Baltimore: Penguin Books, 1954), 98C, p. 157.

49. *Loc. cit.*

50. References are made to "peak experiences" throughout Maslow's writing but particularly in his *Toward a Psychology of Being.* 2nd. Ed. (Princeton: Van Nostrand Press, 1970); *Religions, Values and Peak-Experiences.* (N.Y.: The Viking Press, 1970); and the posthumous work, *The Farther Reaches of Human Nature.* (N.Y.: The Viking Press, 1971).

51. In the "Foreword II" to the 1969 printing of *Psychoanalysis and Religion.* (New Haven: Yale University Press, 1969), Fromm reviews with satisfaction the humanistic renaissance within both the Roman Catholic and Protestant churches. However, he interprets this renewed interest in dialogue with men and women of all backgrounds and traditions as reflecting the attitude that the differences in thought and concepts are of secondary importance to what men feel and experience. In a sense, this observation is true, but I do not think it reflects the importance that belief-systems play in human life and that feeling and belief are more closely aligned than Fromm would recognize. Man is bound by a common humanity, but that is not to say that what he believes is unimportant. Fromm's own intellectual commitment to socialism as an economic and political system would belie his implied view that beliefs are of little importance.

52. Erich Fromm, *Man for Himself.* (N.Y.: Rinehart and Company, Inc., 1947), pp. 44, 45.

53. See Norman Cousins Ed. *'In God We Trust'* (N.Y.: Harper and Brothers, 1958), a very skillfully edited

volume of the religious writings and statements of our Founding Fathers.

54. I have dealt at some length with the metaphysical implications of humanistic psychology in an article, "The Hidden Philosophical Agenda: A Commentary on Humanistic Psychology," *Journal of the American Academy of Religion,* Volume XXXVII, March, 1969, Number 1, pp. 3-14.
55. Revised Standard Version, *The Book of Job,* Chapters 38, 39, 40 (selections).
56. Paul Tillich, *Morality and Beyond* (N.Y.: Harper and Row, 1963) is suggestive of a humanistic and beyond stance regarding the problem we are discussing.
57. The author was in the USSR for six weeks in 1967, visited five Republics and travelled over 10,000 miles. The duplicity of the Soviet's attitudes toward religious art is illustrated by the explanation of the "Madonna and Child" by Leonardo da Vinci in the Hermitage Museum in Leningrad to the effect that it is one of the most beautiful expressions of human love in the history of art, and the inscription beneath a ceramic of The Madonna in the Museum of the History of Religion and Atheism (formerly the Redemption Church) stating that this picture was used by the capitalists to soften the reaction of the masses to the cruelties of human exploitation.
58. Paul Kurtz, "Epilogue: Is Everyone a Humanist?" in Paul Kurtz, Ed. *The Humanist Alternative.* (Buffalo: Prometheus Books, 1973), p. 177.

Chapter IV

The Heuristic Value of a Theistic World-View

The purpose of this chapter is to inquire about the ways in which a theistic world-view informs and illuminates human experience. As we have noted earlier, no experience bears within itself its own meaning. Even the experience of the 'numinous' as a primary datum in man's sense of the 'beyond' has no specificity of meaning until it is placed within a context of meaning through some conscious or unconsciously derived cognitive process. A person may intuitively feel that the 'awesome' nature of his experience is grounded in a reality beyond himself, but as soon as he identifies it as divine or gives it some other appellation, he has raised it above the level of primary experience to a second-order range of cognitive meaning. Theism is a philosophical point of view that attempts to provide a conceptual frame of reference for meaning that will be inclusive and coherent. Obviously, it is not the only philosophical position

146

one might find adequate to explain experience; the history of thought is filled with a wide variety of philosophical views that attempt to interpret experience within some unitary conceptual scheme and make sense out of existence.

The question is: How does a theistic world-view facilitate a comprehensive understanding of man and his universe? By "understanding" I mean more than self-consistent intellectual propositions; rather, I refer to an existential sense of wholeness and meaning that includes both the rational and non-rational aspects of experience. These include man's sensory, moral, aesthetic, religious and social experiences— all that comprise his humanity. One of the central themes of this volume has been the tendency of a naturalistic philosophical perspective to be reductionistic as it attempts to put an empirical and rational handle on human experience. It seems to me that a theistic construct of the meaning of human experience, in all of its depth and richness, provides a more complete understanding of our own personhood and those creative moments in life through which we transcend, at least in part, the limitations imposed by a purely spatio-temporal life perspective.

The Importance of a Conscious World-View

All men have a world-view,[1] but only a few are consciously aware of the factors that enter into their outlook or perspective on life. The term 'world-view,' does not appear in most English dictionaries. In German, a person's *Weltanschauung* refers to his conception of the world, his philosophy of life. The common expression, "reality is as we perceive it to be," reflects the existential fact of the interplay between *how* we look at our world and the world as it is. This is merely another way to state the obvious interaction between the so-called subjective and objective aspects of reality. An individual's world-view is shaped by many cultural and physical influences as he 'reads into' and 'reads out of' his experiences what may or may not be objectively 'there.' A world-view emerges; it does not occur all at once. Man *has* a world-view! The individual does not fully self-determine his outlook on life; at the same time it is not fully determined for him. Otherwise, man could be forever shaped by those environmental forces over which he has no control. The historical fact is that there always seems to be a remnant in society that shakes off, at least in part, the shackles of conformity and voices a perspective on life and values that challenges the status quo and points in a different direction than the prevailing ethos of the time. World-views are both conceptual and non-conceptual, rational and non-rational, personal and communal, intuitive and consciously reflective, that is to say, they are influenced by the totality of one's personal and societal experience.

Most of us would like to believe that how we look at the world, in all of its complexity and ambiguity, is the result of a reflective and contemplative process which comes from weighing all of the pros and cons of each attitude or belief we hold. Pschyoanalytic studies clearly indicate that our attitudes and perceptions about our world are shaped by both preconscious and unconscious forces of which we are not aware. Nonetheless, it is also true that one of the powers of the conscious mind is to transcend immediate experience and take a look, as it were, at those forces that are shaping our world-view and as a consequence construct a more meaningful life-perspective. The challenge is to tap the capacity for freedom each man possesses that will enable him to develop a world-view which he can call his own.

Most people are not conscious of the world-view they live by; their motivations are so mixed and their commitments so vague there is no continuing thread of belief that gives a consistent pattern to their lives. If life is particularly hard

148

and difficult, survival may have the highest value and their world-view will be shaped by the demands of the immediate present. As the consequence, their allegiance will go to whomever will assure their survival. It is at this point that the Communist promise of food, clothing, housing, medical assistance, education and work looks so attractive to those in the third and fourth worlds because it provides basic survival needs.

Parenthetically, democratic political systems may assure freedom to vote, freedom of assembly, freedom of movement, etc., but when they do not assure, at the same time, a humane subsistence level of existence, communal political movements often appeal much more to the person who is suffering from malnutrition and has no place to live or work. Most Americans assume that the Chinese peasant, who is faced with the struggle for physical survival, places the right to vote high on his value agenda. The fact is he is hungry and other human rights are secondary-order values that will naturally emerge when more pressing physical needs are met. Once man has experienced the meaning of freedom, he will often endure all kinds of physical suffering to achieve and work for a higher value, but it is unlikely his world-view will be marked by such idealism if he knows no other value than the primary need for survival.

Within democratic societies our world-view is shaped by an admixture of material and spiritual goals that often conflict with each other. Oftentimes we are a mystery to ourselves and to those with whom we associate. There is no assurance that as the result of self-reflection a consistent life-perspective will emerge, but it is unlikely that without conscious thought such will be the case unless we have been dehumanized by the brain-washing techniques of propaganda. What constitutes the process of developing a conscious world-view in our attempt to make sense out of our experience?

First and foremost is the will to effect changes in life perspective and attitude. Because we are both rational and non-rational beings, some experience of great joy or sorrow, or a personal or collective challenge that forces us to muster all of our energies to meet the crisis, or a particularly enriching experience that is a part of a relationship with a person or persons, may unlock for us new horizons of potential meaning that we want to pursue. We have already commented on the encapsulating effect that limited conceptual perspectives can have upon life. At the same time, clarity of intellectual perspective is essential in the development of a coherent world-view. By coherence I mean a principle that is broader than logical meaning and includes the bi-polar aspects of experience, viewing them as a part of a more unified whole. The principle of *yang/yin,* light/dark, positive/negative, etc. in Chinese thought is a clue to the reality of bi-polarity in human experience. The positive and negative poles in an electrical system are not contradictory elements, but serve in a bi-polar relationship to a single constructive value we call electricity. The intellectual and emotional challenge is to transcend ourselves, through moments of reflection, and objectify our own experiences in an effort to develop consciously a world-view that will serve as positive markers and guides in the forest of life. One does not have to do this alone. Through reading the classical sources in philosophy, religion and literature, one may sift from these statements those insights and principles that ring true to his own experience and, as the result, clarify where he stands as a thoughtful person. The development of a world-view is a process; the meaning is derived in the quest and not in the absolute character of the conceptualization of any one given world-wiew. At the same time, our psychic lives demand some focal frame of reference for meaning that bears within itself some consistency; otherwise, we would fall apart and end in nihilism. In addition, many people find, in their own subcultures, other persons who share the same quest for meaning and in their mutual experience grow in positive ways together.

As the result of conscious reflection, one may come to the conclusion that all is absurd and that meaning in life is only momentary, at best, and that the acceptance of absurdity is the only reasonable stance to take. This, too is a world-view and a life-perspective. It is no happenstance that most of twentieth-century literature is dominated by the theme that man's attempt to find cosmic meaning in a meaningless universe is futile. This mood has been prompted by the disillusionment of World War I and the heinous depth to which man can sink as illustrated by the holocaust of World War II. Man's life is filled with paradox: he seeks immortality through his creative endeavors only to be reminded daily of his mortality; he seeks all knowledge only to discover that his knowledge is relative; he desires complete fulfillment only to realize that he can only be partially fulfilled. His world-view is marked by hardheaded realism; he will not flinch from the challenge of the encounter though he knows rationally he can never win. As in the case of Albert Camus, he may find personal integrity and satisfaction in his rebellion. What keeps him going? It may be the "will to live," both physically and psychologically; he settles for the *struggle itself* and beyond that there is no meaning. He may wish there were something worth preserving in the struggle and this may be an unconscious force in his motivational life because of the Jewish and Christian ethos of which he is a part, but he denies it as a conscious principle. His world-view is not abstract or theoretical—it is pragmatic and functional. Simply stated, for him "the purpose of life is to get through it." [2]

There is little question that such a life perspective performs an informative role as one approaches human relationships and other aspects of experience. At least, one does not expect too much from life and is grateful for what little meaning or value he might find. Whether or not there is a better way is an open question. At best it is a courageous life-stance because it refuses to accept the easy answer that might be emotionally appealing, but does not stand the test of man's deepest experiences. Casting this posture within the terminology of this essay, it is a kind of negative naturalism that makes no positive affirmations about metaphysical reality; it settles for the here and now. It is not humanistic, in terms of the *Humanist Manifesto II* statement examined earlier in this volume, because it does not share the humanist faith that through reason and the application of new knowledge to human problems we can improve the human condition in significant ways on this planet. The philosophy of the absurd finds no grounds for a positive hope; yet, it refuses to be nihilistic because on the deepest level of consciousness it seeks new experiences that may enrich one's life.

The reason I have cited this form of philosophical perspective is because it is more dominant within the intellectual community than most people realize. When it becomes a way of life and develops into a life-style, it becomes self-confirming and entrenched as the norm for all persons of supposed sophistication and insight. Alienation is seen no longer as a descriptive psychological condition, but is viewed as a metaphysical reality normatively characteristic of all human existence. If one does not feel alienated in the depths of his being, he is somehow naive or non-reflective, because from this point of view, it is inconceivable that any person who thinks deeply could not feel the same way about his existence. Or if a person believes that he has transcended his alienated condition through God's forgiveness or grace, this is viewed as a form of self-deception. When such notions become fixed within human consciousness, all experience is seen in this light and shapes the person's world-view. From my point of view, knowing what one's world-view is and some understanding of how it has developed in one's life, is of great importance, because only as we become conscious of its import in our lives can we evaluate it critically and determine its conceptual and existential adequacy. Let us now examine a theistic perspective of life, meaning and value.

What Is Theism?

The hangups that men and women in our age have with the word "God" is understandable in the light of the many powers and acts attributed to him. Even a cursory glance at the church page of any American newspaper will reveal the claims that religious people and their leaders make for what God can and will do for mankind. These affirmations range from the bizarre to the more psychologically oriented position of what faith can accomplish as one becomes attuned to the "God" within each person. The appeals come in many forms; the assurances and promises for a better life here and in the life to come are reassuring; and the authoritative source for these claims is said to be not of this world. As a result, the anxieties that arise in times of trouble are exploited and people are intimidated to believe. When primarily emotional appeals are made to effect responses of belief, coupled with all of the contemporary devices the secular world uses to sell toothpaste, it takes a strong person to resist such techniques; thus he often believes no matter how incredible the belief might be. When a thoughtful person confronts this kind of appeal in the name of 'God' it is no wonder he is turned off and finds more creatively profitable things to think about.

In addition, God is often seen as the Big X or the Great

Unknown that science cannot deal with; hence as science advances in its understanding of man and the physical universe the power and significance of the Big X diminishes. Though naturalistic theism—a term we will define later— does hold to certain views of man and the universe, it is not a point of view competing with scientific investigation. Rather, the language of theistic religion is in the form of symbols that open up to man deeper levels of understanding which, in principle, science cannot explore. Theistic belief does not consist of "factual" statements but instead is an interpretation of man's experience with his world that is metaphysically significant. Theistic faith is concerned with another dimension of meaning than is provided by only a spatial and temporal understanding of man and nature. It finds purely naturalistic philosophical postulates too restrictive—a theme I have emphasized throughout this essay.

Theistic belief has a rich history and meaning that can provide a positive heuristic function in the guidance we all seek in understanding our lives. A theistic world-view, as a postulational construct, may help us place our experiences into a more adequate frame of reference of meaning. What is involved in a theistic world-view? No one knows the origin of religion, but a brief historical statement regarding the emergence of the idea of God might be helpful.

Perhaps the earliest sense of an "Other" power occurred in man's experience with natural forces he could not understand. This *pre-animistic* stage arose as an undifferentiated sense of fear was evoked by earthquakes, lightning, volcanic eruptions, heavenly disturbances, and the like. As the result, primitive man sought to placate the forces that caused these events and cowed in fear before them. Reductionistic approaches to forms of worship that relate man to the mysterious forces of nature would suggest that the basic motivation for all religious responses to the world is founded upon fear and superstition of the unknown. Unquestionably there are remnants of primitive superstitions in all of us, but to suggest that religion is primarily a fear-response to the tyranny of an unpredictable god or gods in nature is to fail to distinguish qualitatively between the fear of primitive man and the appropriate responses of awe and reverence that Nature inspires among men and women in our own time. The danger of the genetic fallacy, suggested in our brief discussion on the impact of Darwin's thought, is relevant.

The next higher level of man's 'religious' response to nature is *animism*. Here spiritual beings or forces are identified as somehow innate within physical objects. Oesterley and Robinson [3] suggest that it is no happenstance that trees, running water and stones play a significant role in the religious life of early Judaism. People saw these objects move; since they neither understood the law of gravitation nor the principles of growth they attributed these changes to an animating force or spirit. Parenthetically, it was the work of Isaac Newton (1642-1727) that marked the end of animism in what we now call inanimate objects and, in fact, marked the beginning of challenging the nature of the spiritual aspect of man's nature.

Closely related to animism is *magic* in which physical objects are infused with supernatural powers, such as the rod of Moses that performs all kinds of unexplainable things.

Polytheism develops as the belief in the activity of many gods, all performing functions appropriate to their nature and mission. The Greek pantheon of gods, the gods of the Canaanites, Babylonians and Assyrians are illustrations of this stage of man's religious beliefs and extend to the worship of astral deities in fairly recent times. From a practical standpoint, identifying a god with a particular function he could be depended upon to perform had its merits because it made more concrete the god's function than attributing all things to a single deity, as in the case of monotheism.

Whether or not it meets the cognitive need for a unitary principle by which the whole of experience can be explained is another matter. But purely from a practical and simplistic point of view, polytheistic beliefs supplied the answers for felt needs in the life of people throughout history.

The point at which *theism* emerges on the historical scene is difficult to determine. There is some evidence that as early as the time of Ikhnaton (Amenhotep IV) of Egypt (c. 1375 B.C.) the god Aton was viewed as the father of all mankind and the universal governing principle of all things. This is not monotheism in full bloom, but it is a precursor of a central idea that emerged later within Judaism in which the universe is conceived as expressive of a single, unitary power. *Monotheism,* in contrast to henotheistic belief in the superior power of one God over other gods, affirms the existence of one single unitary Reality that is the Ground and Source of all that exists. This Reality is self-existent, non-contingent and infinite. It is the *alpha* and the *omega,* the beginning and end of all that is. Thus, the perennial question of who created God is excluded by definition because God is that behind which one cannot go. Infinity extends many ways: an eternity of time before, within, and after the present—connecting space not only beyond us, but inside of us. God is both transcendent and immanent; that is, He is both beyond the commonly accepted "limits" of the space-time world, yet He expresses himself within the natural order. In contrast to *deism,* which stresses the transcendent character of deity who created the world and set it in its orderly pattern only to leave it forever alone, and distinguishable from *pantheism* in which nature is equated with God (God is everywhere), theism combines both the transcendent and immanent character of God into one concept.

The common problem of literally identifying God's place

and location as "here" or "there," "up" or "down," "outside" or "inside" is inevitable when we ascribe His activity to any specific time or place. Hume's attack upon analogous forms of expression as necessarily in error and the fact that the infinite cannot be in any way comparable to the finite merely affirms that we are caught on the horns of a linguistic dilemma that is inescapable. Thinking of God as the symbol of that unity we find in the realm of our personal and collective experience, enables us to speak of God without being guilty of making our symbols literal referents of that toward which they point. It is the idolatry of both word and deed that has bred religious exclusivism and bigotry—the greatest enemies of any search for truth. We often refer to realms of experience that cannot be spatially or temporally identified. We speak of our true selves, or the sense of personal presence we feel in another person, or refer to other non-spatial aspects of our conscious experience that are more than figments of the imagination and upon which we place a great deal of importance. Perhaps the human experience that illustrates a transcendent dimension is that of self-transcendence. In an instant of time we can look at what occurred yesterday, what is happening at this moment, and what might take place tomorrow. In a sense, we are standing outside of ourselves in a moment of self-conscious awareness. Consequently, we speak of the mind's ability to rise above bodily existence and poetically speak of this as the life of the mind or spirit. As our minds and consciousness have no location, expressions such as the mind is *in* us or *outside* us seem inappropriate forms of language, though we often use these forms of expression.

From the theistic point of view, God is not only transcendent and immanent, he is also conscious will and intelligence. The idea of the Covenant in both Judaism and Christianity is predicated upon the assumption that God, as Person, can enter into a covenant with persons. From this understanding God is seen as morally dependable in contrast to the capricious character of the gods within conventional polytheistic religions. Here God is identified with moral attributes and becomes a symbol of man's highest duty. His moral will is expressed throughout the history of both Judaism and Christianity. The Law of Moses, the teachings of the 8th century prophets of Israel that love of God is inseparably related to human concern for justice, love and righteousness, as well as Jesus' summarization of the Law as love to neighbor and to God, all set a standard for human conduct and life. This model of the moral life and man's highest duties provides a moral frame of reference for man and *informs* his experience concerning good and bad, right and wrong. Granted, these "objective" values are filtered through our own cultural understanding and only appear to us in their pure forms in rare moments of history, yet when man believes that his highest moral duty is rooted in the nature of God himself, it not only clarifies his conceptual understanding of what the good is, but also performs a practical function in guiding his daily life. The familiar phrase, "to do the Will of God," implies an objective ground for a sense of moral obligation that has been a powerful force within the life of man. God becomes the symbol and source for the highest Good.

But perhaps the primary conceptual value the theistic understanding of the universe has provided is its attempt to "answer" a fundamental problem raised in ancient Greek philosophy, namely, identity *and* change, being *and* becoming, unity *and* plurality, cosmos *and* chaos. One of Plato's conceptions of the function of the divine in the creative process was to bring order out of chaos.[4] For example, Heraclitus as well as the Stoics saw the universe as guided by the principle of *logos* (reason) that gave stability and order to all things. This was a metaphysical principle that provided unity to that which was in flux and change.

As our psyche cannot survive and realize its potential when it is split and torn asunder by chaos, neither can the world survive unless it functions in accord with those laws that are appropriate to itself. The theistic construct provides a symbolic framework that serves a needed unitary ontological ground for understanding the universe of which we are a part. In spite of the pluralistic aspects of our experience in and with the world, we still call it a cosmos and a universe, and not a chaos or a multiverse. The problem of the one and the many, as old as Parmenides' philosophy, still plagues us. It seems to me that a theistic world-view illumines this problem.

Forms of Theistic Belief

The wide spectrum of beliefs flying under the banner of a theistic point of view is confusing to the layman who often assumes that if one believes in God there is a commonality of understanding about God's nature and his relationship to man and the world. Fortunately, such is not the case; if there were uniformity of belief about the nature of deity, theology would be a dull discipline. Speculative theology is an enticing intellectual activity; its history, represented by some of the greatest minds of the ages, is full, rich and profound. Unhappily, few laymen read the writings of the great theologians of the past or the present; rather they receive their impression of the theological enterprise from the dogmatic proclamations they hear in the pulpit or on the air. There is nothing like a good course in philosophy of religion or theology to soften the antagonism of those who believe that the study of theology is without intellectual substance.

There are many types of theism expressed in a wide variety of philosophical and institutional forms. We have arbitrarily chosen some contemporary expressions of theistic belief most likely to be found in the religious community in order to help the layperson identify the theistic perspective from which a minister or religious teacher may be speaking. If the theological ear is trained, the listener can soon detect the theistic framework from which a person is expounding his interpretations of God's relationship to man and the world. The problem is that most people have so little intellectual sophistication in these matters that they are prone to take on face value whatever their clergyman or religious teacher tells them. Seldom is their response based upon reflection and knowledge. This is not unique to religion. We tend to listen to whomever we accept as an authority figure. Rejection of religious teachings might equally be non-reflective and prejudiced. As the nominal believer may accept uncritically what his religion tells him, the unbeliever can be just as uncritical in rejecting out of hand religious interpretations merely because they are "religious." This type of negative response is often based upon a stereotype of "religion" that can be as naively grounded as its counterpart. With this problem in mind, the following index of current theistic beliefs may help the reader sift out the perspective from which certain religious statements are being made.

It appears to me that there are at least four major theological perspectives within the Christian understanding that have profoundly shaped contemporary religious thought and have a bearing upon the individual's religious worldview. Where one stands within this spectrum of belief will have a significant relationship to an understanding of himself and his universe of meaning. These theistic positions are: Classical or Conservative Supernaturalism (Orthodoxy); Radical Supernaturalism (Fundamentalism); Neo-Supernaturalism (Neo-Orthodoxy); Naturalistic Theism (Liberalism). I recognize that these are arbitrary delineations.[5] Theologians, like other people, do not want to be pigeonholed into some arbitrary category, but I do think that identifying belief-systems with broad strokes is a useful conceptual device for clarifying beliefs. Many of these distinctions could apply to Jewish belief systems as well, but our focus is primarily upon Christian theism.

(1) Classical or Conservative Supernaturalism (Orthodoxy.[6]

Orthodox religion stresses the revelations that God has made of himself through the Church, the Bible and nature. Its authority is predicated upon the unique and special ways God has manifested himself to the world and most dramatically and especially in the person of Jesus Christ. From an orthodox point of view, it is argued that there is a common thread of interpretation throughout Christian history that reveals the nature of God to man through those special instruments God has chosen to make clear his will for man. Thus the "Word (Christ) within the Word (the Bible)" becomes the clue to God's nature. Orthodoxy emphasizes the importance of the major figures in Christian thought who have interpreted the meaning of God's message for man. Since the intellectual posture of orthodoxy is within the scholarly western tradition, these interpretations are studied in the light of those intellectual influences that have played a role in shaping their thought. For example, Augustine's unique attempt to blend Manicheism, Neo-Platonism, Jewish and classical Greek categories of thought into a Christian world-view, is of interest to orthodox scholars as they try to understand the shaping of a Christian understanding of man and history. Orthodox theologians begin with the axiom of God's existence and accept, as a part of the *given,* God's revelation to man. Their task is to clarify the meaning of that revelation as it pertains to man's salvation and redemption. The classical expressions of faith in the Creeds, the theological writings of the Early Church Fathers, the Scholastics, the Reformers and those that followed are focal points of reference. For Protestants, the Bible is the key source for God's revelation of himself while for the Roman and Greek traditions of Catholicism, the teachings of the Church as well as the Bible are viewed as authoritative referents.

Orthodoxy stresses the natural *and* the supernatural. Since God is seen as omniscient, omnipotent, holy, just and righteous, God is the Lord of history and all life. God discloses himself from *outside* the world *into* the world through his "mighty acts"—seen as "signs," "wonders," and "powers." Therefore, his ways are beyond human understanding, and acts of divine intervention are evidence of his divine will acting *upon* this world. Within the major stream of Roman Catholic theology, the distinction between revealed and natural theology is closely drawn. What God reveals to man cannot be understood fully by man's natural reason, though man can find a belief in God a reasonable claim because of the "evidences" for God's existence in the natural order. Revealed truths are manifest through Christ, the Bible and the doctrines and teachings of the Church as well as in the divine virtues of faith, hope and love. The emphasis is upon divine *and* natural truth; divine revelation complements ordinary knowledge and any conflict between the two realms of truth are only apparent, because God, as the source for all truth, cannot contradict the unity of his own being and nature. Similar emphasis in Protestant circles stresses God as the source for revealed truth, but greater emphasis is placed upon the Bible and the witness of the historic Christian community to Jesus as the Savior, than in the Roman and Eastern wings of the Christian tradition. Both Protestant and Catholic traditions empha-

162

size man's sinfulness and need for redemption. They are both sacramental religions—the Protestants viewing baptism and the eucharist as sacraments—the Catholics, in addition, accepting the sacraments of ordination, confirmation, extreme unction, matrimony and penance. Tradition, the witness of the believing community throughout the ages, the centrality of Christ as God's supreme expression of Himself to man, the doctrines and creeds, dramatized in a wide variety of liturgical forms, are all a part of the richness of an orthodox person's world-view. He sees life within a divine framework of meaning and purpose of which he is a part and finds the rationale for his existence within that scheme and understanding of things. When such a perspective becomes his living stance and more than an intellectual affirmation, he finds it a source for strength and courage in facing the vicissitudes of life. It is this faith that undergirds the whole of his existence and performs both a conceptual and existential function.

Orthodox Christians vary in their emphasis upon the priority of personal religious experience. The evangelical revival that spread through England and this country in the 18th century was a unique combination of orthodoxy and a type of personal-salvation religion with all of its emotional revivalistic overtones. The concern has been for the substance of a religious experiential encounter with God through Christ as a safeguard against the formal liturgical patterns becoming a substitute for personal religious experience. Today evangelical groups [7] are combining into a unique synthesis the importance of orthodox doctrinal beliefs rooted in the main stream of the Christian tradition, and a personally vital religious experience—what John Wesley called "the warm heart." Within this movement is a serious regard for theological and historical scholarship as it attempts to resurrect orthodoxy from its sterile and cold

163

tradition. The charismatic movement within Roman Catholicism and Anglicanism are cases in point, as well as similar emphases within the main line Protestant churches.

(2) Radical Supernaturalism (Fundamentalism) [8]

Fundamentalism is predominantly an American Protestant phenomenon that arose as a reaction to the social gospel liberalism of the early part of this century. Its roots are in orthodoxy, but it is orthodoxy overly simplified; thus it has been a popular movement among those who want to find emotional satisfaction in their religion without encumbering it with a complex theological structure that is rooted in a somewhat ambiguous theological history. By and large it is insensitive to scholarship—stresses the immediacy of Christ's presence in life and emphasizes the experiential aspects of orthodox Christianity without many of the liturgical or ritualistic trappings. Regarding the Bible, it tends to be literalistic and holds to the notion that the original monographs were directly inspired by God through human instruments. It makes Pauline theological categories normative and attempts to base its authority upon the historical witness of the apostolic community. It is crisis-oriented in its view of conversion and sees God as continuing to perform miracles in the lives of men and women. It bases its authority not only upon the witness of the apostolic community but also upon the factual historicity of the Biblical accounts of divine intervention in the forms of miraculous events that appear to contradict the natural order. It looks upon the Bible as the source for all truth that is necessary for salvation and Christ as the sacrificial gift of God to man. Though God expresses his nature through the physical world, the emphasis is upon God revealing himself to man from outside the world of space and time. Its strength is in the self-confirming nature of personal experience with

God through Christ, and it is primarily upon this foundation of truth that it makes its claim. It is a two-world view, God standing over against the world to judge the world and at the same time to redeem the world. Its objective is to evangelize the world. It tends to be exclusive in its truth-claim and believes that God's revelation of Himself in Jesus Christ is normative for all other claims for truth. Its impact upon the masses is great, particularly in times of severe distress and difficulty; its assurances are positive and absolute; and its other-worldly appeal is particularly attractive to those who find this life filled with disillusionment and disappointment. It is definite and explicitly prescriptive concerning matters of conduct and choice; it demands full and complete allegiance; and without question has been a transforming force within the life of millions of people. Its stress upon the folly of man's wisdom tends to minimize the significance or value of social reform movements; its hope is in the eschaton when the full realization of God's purposes for man will be fulfilled. Parenthetically, renewed interest in a theology of the last days (the eschaton) has developed within orthodox circles during the past few years; but by and large, this emphasis has been left to fundamentalistically-oriented evangelical groups.

The problem that many theists and non-theists find with supernaturalism generally is in its claim that God's intervention, in the form of miracles that appear to violate what we believe to be nature's laws, are viewed as historical facts. I refer specifically to the Biblical accounts of crossing the Red Sea, the tablets given to Moses by God on Mt. Sinai, the sun standing still, the virgin birth of Jesus, the raising of Lazarus from the dead, the physical resurrection of Jesus and similar accounts of historical events. If it is assumed that "with God all things are possible," in the literal sense, then an omnipotent God is not limited by anything whatever. If on the other hand, the laws of nature are seen as

165

expressions of God's order within the natural process, a point of view we will develop in our discussion of naturalistic theism, then to set aside arbitrarily a natural law would violate one aspect of God's nature. Unfortunately, a critically historical and comparative study of the Biblical accounts was not undertaken from the time of Origen in the 3rd century A.D. to the scholarly investigations of the Biblical critics in the 19th century. By and large, it was assumed the Biblical accounts were historically true records of man's origins and history. When it is recognized that the Biblical accounts were written in an age rampant with supernatural claims for all kinds of events [9] and in a time when man did not think of natural causal connections between events, the Biblical stories can be placed in some kind of historical and social perspective that places these accounts within their pre-scientific setting. In addition, Judaism and Christianity are not the only religions that make supernatural claims for events within their traditions; to suggest that supernatural events recorded within the Bible differ from similar events claimed by other traditions, is to portray a God that is arbitrary in performing 'miracles' for one people and not another.

It seems to me that supernatural forms of theism do not face the full implication of a post-Copernican world-view and that there is an inevitable conflict between science and religion when religion begins to talk dogmatically about what did or did not occur, or when it makes factual claims for phenomena that cannot be tested by the commonly accepted canons of what constitutes likely or probable fact. We have already suggested that one of the ways out of this dilemma is to view religious historical interpretations of reality as mythological, symbolic and poetic expressions of a deeper insight and truth about reality than alleged historical events can provide. This approach runs counter to the main stream of orthodox teachings that places its authoritative claim upon the historicity of the events recorded within the tradition. If an individual says, "The resurrection of Jesus from the dead is my faith," there can be no argument, but if he states, "The resurrection of Jesus from the dead is a fact," then it seems to me that such an assertion must stand the test of the historiographer's examination of that claim.

Our disagreement with the positivistic contention concerning what is a verifiable proposition or what is not verifiable, is not over the identification of such propositions with factual statements; rather, it is the implication that reality can be limited to empirically verifiable propositions, thus bracketing out metaphysical and theological statements as having any other than subjective significance. The issues here are complex and my own position is not without problems, but it appears quite clear to me that the great stumbling block for people who have been educated and conditioned by a scientifically oriented world-view is to accept the presuppositions upon which a supernatural theism is based. I will present later in this chapter a naturalistic theistic view and I will try to show that the conflict between naturalism and supernaturalism can be resolved. Naturalistic theism presses farther than a purely naturalistic perspective is willing to go into its understanding of reality.

(3) Neo-Supernaturalism (Neo-Orthodoxy) [10]

Neo-Orthodoxy first took roots on the Continent during the 1920's as a reaction to the overly optimistic views of the liberal movement in theology that extended from the 19th century through World War I, that the Kingdom of God could be brought about upon this earth if enough men and women were dedicated to love and care for their fellow

167

man, as they saw perfect love expressed in the life and teachings of Jesus of Nazareth. It was a reaction against a superficial humanism with the halo of a loosely defined Christian faith. The disillusionment that followed World War I and the designs of the Nazi movement in the 30's shook the overly simplistic faith in man's inherent goodness—a central notion within liberal theological circles. In addition, the liberal movement reduced Jesus to an ethical teacher and doer of good and placed him within the Jewish prophetic tradition as a uniquely inspired human being, but not the Son of God of the Biblical tradition. For neo-orthodox thinkers, this removed the essence of the Christian message from its central place in history and made Jesus another religious leader who had no special claim upon the life of mankind.

At the same time, neo-orthodoxy could not return to the pure supernaturalism of an earlier orthodoxy because it accepted the scholarly work of the Biblical and historical critics of the 19th century as relevant to a responsible understanding of the Bible and, of course, it had been influenced in its world-view by the impact of scientific knowledge in the past four hundred years of western intellectual history. Therefore, it was a *new* orthodoxy in the sense that it recognized the important contributions that secular scholarship had made to an understanding of our lives and the traditions that surround them; yet, at the same time it was orthodox in its emphasis upon God's acts in history as focal points of God's revelation of Himself. The miracles were not stressed as the rationale and justification for the authenticity of the Gospel's message; rather, stress was placed upon the meaning and symbolic value of what Christ meant to the historic Christian community.

At first, orthodox theologians rejoiced that orthodoxy had been rediscovered but when they realized that, by and large, neo-orthodox scholars were viewing God's acts in a symbolic and not a literal way, they began to see that there were fundamental differences in their understanding of their common theological heritage. The neo-orthodox emphasis was upon the *message* within the Bible and not its factuality. It believed that the myth of the Fall of Man portrays the true condition of man and that the redemptive message of the Gospel points toward the reality of a God of Love. It endeavored to re-establish the roots of Christianity within the richness of the theological tradition and emphasized the insights and relevance of Christian theologians throughout the ages, particularly the Reformers of the 16th century. It had a salutary effect upon the revitalization of the Christian community toward the essential teachings and doctrines that have characterized the faith of the Church through the ages. At the same time, it tried to incorporate contemporary scholarship into its theological and historical perspective. It chastened the facile liberal and challenged the orthodox wedded to an unexamined tradition. It declared its posture as confessional, without apology, and thus avoided the conflicts created by the attempt to defend the historicity of either the Biblical account or the events surrounding it. It acknowledged the importance of the renewal of faith in the Lord of history and affirmed the heuristic value of this faith as it informs man about the reality of his contingency and proclivity toward *hubris,* or pride, as that which separates man from man, and man from God. It relied upon the authoritative character of the truth of faith within the historic witnessing community. It found the Kierkegaardian emphasis upon faith, as arising out of man's sense of hopelessness and despair for bringing about his own salvation, as faithful to the Biblical emphasis upon faith as the gift of God to man. It was a supernaturalistic theism without the impediments of a strict orthodoxy. It influenced the theological perspectives of the main line churches and is a theological point of view that is prevalent among theologians today.

(4) Naturalistic Theism (Liberalism) [11]

It is with some degree of hesitancy that I link naturalistic theism with "liberalism," because many thinkers who have contributed to this perspective would not like to be so classified. Nonetheless, the movement has been liberal and non-supernatural in the sense that it was profoundly influenced by evolution and the notion that reality is one organic whole.

Also, it has consistently stressed the personal experiential aspects of life as the ultimate criterion for meaning and suggests that the word 'empirical' should include subjective experience as a part of the data as well as so-called objective experience. Thus it is an empirical philosophy of religion. It rejects the two-world view of all forms of supernaturalism, previously outlined; thus it is close to philosophical naturalism, though it insists that natural processes are best seen as expressions of the divine purpose operating within them. As a result, the emphasis is upon the immanence of God within the natural and historical process in contrast to God revealing himself *to* the world *from* outside the world. From this point of view, the line between what is secular and divine, or what is divine and human is difficult to draw. Likewise inspiration and revelation are viewed as characteristic of those experiences in human life that raise human consciousness to higher levels of appreciation and understanding and disclose something about reality that has not previously been discovered. It sees God as the source of all good and finds the holy in the secular and ordinary. Obviously there is the possibility that the naturalistic theist is "reading in" what is not in reality there, but as we have pointed out repeatedly in this essay this is a problem for anyone who seriously investigates the epistemological situation. That which uplifts the human spirit and raises man above the sordid and petty aspects of life is seen as the divine operative within the natural order. God is not limited in the 'revelation' of himself to the sanctuary or the cloister but he is a part of aesthetic, moral and social experiences that pull us toward beauty, goodness and love.

Some years ago a student came up to me on the campus about a problem of racial discrimination; his concern was deep and serious. After our discussion, I privately responded with personal thankfulness that God was expressing his moral nature within the deeply felt convictions of this young man. I am confident that if I had shared my understanding of our conversation with him, he would have replied, "Why bring God into it? It is merely a matter of right over against wrong!" From the naturalistic theistic perspective, it was more than that; his concern was prompted by an ontologically rooted principle within himself and the universe of which it is a part. When that which is good for mankind is identified with the immanent expression of God's activity in human experience, then the discovery of polio vaccine, or any other achievement that contributes to a higher level of human good, is the divine operative within the so-called natural world. Here the values of humanism are linked with the world-view of theism. Humanism, by definition, need not be only naturalistic.

In addition, naturalistic humanistic theism stresses the authority of reason, conscience and intuition over creeds, doctrines and ecclesiastical systems. It sees life as a cooperative adventure involving man with man, and man with God. It does not expect God to intervene in some supernatural way in man's behalf but emphasizes the importance of human knowledge, intelligence and will in understanding more adequately the physical and natural laws that are conducive to human wellbeing and as expressive of the divine will for man. It shares with self-realization humanism the responsibility of man to fulfill his highest and most noble human potential, but disagrees with a humanistic philosophy that does not see this potential as a part of the divine purpose within human existence.

In regard to the many religions of the world that seek a relationship with the Absolute or God, naturalistic theism views these as products of man's universal and natural attempt to find cosmic meaning for life. It believes in the universality of a spiritual reality that is greater than nature and the major religious traditions as human attempts to express what this reality might be in cultural forms that are indigenously related to their own history. Thus each religion has its own unique identity and at the same time is a part of a greater universal whole to which it attempts to relate. This does not mean that all religions are the same or that one is not to be preferred over another, particularly if a humanistic model is believed to be a part of the ontological nature of things, but it does not declare certain religions as false and others true in some absolute sense. It holds a kind of *reverent agnosticism* regarding any claim to absolute truth; yet, it believes that some insight into truth is possible. The same problem I have repeatedly brought up in this volume regarding the dilemma concerning human knowledge and the reality of the interplay between man's relative subjective posture in an objective world holds equally in this case. Yet naturalistic theism does find it necessary to make some claims about what reality might be as it seeks to develop a frame of reference for meaning that will be both conceptually and experientially satisfying. I shall now turn to some specific areas of experience that, from my point of view, are illumined by a naturalistic theistic structure of meaning.

Granting there is no sure proof for God's existence or non-existence, the question still persists as a viable issue because of man's innate curiosity about himself and the nature of the universe in which he lives. Scientific concern for a description of nature's functions dominates scientific interest and whether or not science presses for further answers to other kinds of questions depends, to a large extent, upon the intellectual interests of the scientist himself. Seeking evidence to substantiate one's philosophical views is dangerous business, because there is the tendency to select the data that confirm one's suspicion about *why* nature functions as it does. If an individual is predisposed to an atheistic world-view, the chaotic aspects of nature's ways will loom large in shaping his notions about the nature of physical reality. On the other hand, if a person feels a part of a natural order that is guided by a purposive principle or being, he will have the tendency to see the constructive aspect of the order of things. This is not to suggest that the religious problem is purely autobiographical; it is only to admit the obvious fact that how we see our world—the existential glasses through which we look at reality—profoundly affects the conceptualization we give to our experience. The question we are discussing cannot be answered dogmatically. However, for many lay and professional philosophers, a theistic world-view informs our understanding of the physical universe. We must recognize, at the outset, that the universe should be viewed as a whole, that is, as an integrated unity, the parts of which are aspects of a greater cosmic process. This is a kind of *Gestalt.* As I have pointed out in briefly commenting on the philosophy of Henri Bergson, when one aspect of reality is lifted out of its contextual setting, what is perceived in its isolation from the continuum of which it is a part is a distorted segment of a larger whole. Such a holistic approach is anathema to the scientific mentality that insists upon the isolation of experience—breaking reality down into smaller and smaller units for examination and study. This was the major problem that humanistic psychologists had with behavioristic and experimental approaches to a study of man.[12] Humanists maintained that man must be studied as an organic unity as he experiences his world. We are all plagued with seeing only a part of the picture. Regarding the problem of whether or not there is a purposive element in the physical universe which points toward higher levels of order and value, Peter Bertocci appropriately warns, "Center on one half of the evidence and you become an atheist. Center on the other half and you become a theistic absolutist. Take both together *without any explanatory hypothesis* and you become a skeptic." [13] (Italics mine.) The task of the philosopher of religion is to provide a postulational frame of reference (an hypothesis) that appears to be faithful to human experience. It is our view that a theistic world-view illumines our experience of the world.

The story of the evolutionary creative process is a marvelous account indeed covering a span of billions of years. Man's affinity with nature in both his negative and positive responses is a part of the soil out of which religion developed. There is little question that primitive man's response to nature derived from fear, but this does not mean that man cannot respond to nature in ways that enhance his life perspective. I refer to the beauties of nature and the intricacies of its own processes from simple to complex forms that inspire men to a more sensitive understanding of themselves and their continuity with all forms of physical existence. The emergence of the organic from the inorganic and on to the most complicated levels of existence in mind and consciousness—unique attributes of man—portrays a picture of immense philosophical import. *Why* is nature as it is? Is it a telic process? Is the progression from simple to complex also a progression from lower to higher? What is the most reasonable hypothesis to explain what appears to be a more orderly than disorderly process?

As impressive as man's achievements are, he does not order the world to be what it is; he is neither the creator of the world nor is he the creative principle upon which the future design of nature rests. He may interfere with that design to the extent that it can no longer function, but he is not the efficient cause for what is the *given* within the natural order. As Harlow Shapley points out, "Man in his vaunted superiority is but a minute though interesting detail in the cosmic opera wherein we all play minor parts." [14] Note Shapley did not say "comic opera," as some would see it.

It is not my purpose to present all of the arguments for the existence of God, but I think it is informative to mention the argument from design that has been one of the central philosophical attempts to relate God's existence and function to the natural processes of nature. We find the design argument appearing as early as Cicero's *De Natura Deorum* based upon the regularity of the motion and revolution of the heavens in contrast to the view that the order of the heavens is the result of chance. The Final Cause of Aristotle, toward which nature moves in its path from potentiality to actuality, and Aquinas' fifth argument for the existence of God, namely, "natural bodies act for an end (and) achieve their end, not fortuitously, but designedly," [15] are early expressions of forms of the teleological argument. In the 17th and 18th centuries the argument reappeared with the development of the descriptive natural sciences, particularly biology and astronomy. In recent times, developments in physics, as well as new discoveries in nuclear biology and evolutionary theory, have fostered speculative theistic explanations for the phenomena of nature. First, let us look at the argument from design from the perspective of an 18th century figure, and then from a few 20th century writers.

William Paley was born shortly after Hume's famous *Treatise of Human Nature* appeared and in the time of the evangelical revival in England that was sweeping the country. He sought a rationale for faith that was between the skepticism of Hume and the tendency toward the nonrational in the emotionalism of evangelical revivalism. He was a student at Cambridge University where he was a Fellow. His major work, *Natural Theology* or *Evidences of the Existence and Attributes of the Deity Collected from the Appearances of Nature* was published in 1802, three years before his death.[16] What is the essence of his argument?

His thought falls into two major parts. (1) He contrasts the nature of a watch with a stone in an attempt to illustrate the principle of order and design and (2) he tries to demonstrate the attributes of God as the designer. It is obvious that a watch, as the product of human design, is quite different from a stone which is an inanimate object having no perceptible moving parts to activate some intended function or purpose. In the light of present day physics, a stone is a more complex unit of existence than Paley surmised, but nonetheless the two objects are quite different in both appearance and function. The intended function of a watch is to indicate time. The watch did not just occur or happen; it was the product of someone's intention and design. This does not mean that trial and error were not a part of unlocking the secret of what would make a watch work, but the direction of the search for the clue to developing an instrument that would give the hour of the day was the result of a human decision and not the result of pure fortuitous chance. Whoever invented the watch did not throw into the air pieces of metal in the form of wheels, springs and screws that eventuated in a watch; rather, he arranged these and many other parts into a configuration that would produce the results he intended. Paley uses this analogy to illustrate what he thought to be the character of the natural order and suggests that the same manifestation of design which appears in a watch also appears in nature. He further argues that the cosmic designer, as in the case of an individual who designs a watch or any other object, must be personal, since the qualities of personhood are consciousness, purpose and volition. This classical expression of a teleological world-view which involves a belief in a personal God, who functions as both a transcendent and immanent principle in relationship to nature, is not without its present day exponents. There is a fundamental difference, however, between Paley's approach and that of today's teleologists: Paley believed he could prove God's existence by appealing to the natural order. In contrast, most philosophical theologians defend a teleological understanding of the world as a "reasonable belief," and not as a coercive rational argument. In other words, is it more reasonable to assume that the universe, as we know its evolutionary development, has taken place by chance, or is it just as reasonable, or perhaps more sensible, to affirm that it is essentially purposive in nature when seen from a holistic point of view? Recognizing the indeterminate and unpredictable aspects of nature, many religious philosophers argue from a "wider teleological" point of view in which the homeostatic process and ecobalance within nature is seen as indicating greater purpose and direction than their opposite.

F. R. Tennant reflects this approach when he defends the empirical legitimacy of the claim that the progressive evolution of the processes of nature, from lower to higher forms, can be best understood if an immanent metaphysical principle is postulated as an aspect of the process as a whole. In commenting on Darwin's theory of evolution, Tennant states, "The survival of the fittest presupposes the arrival of the fit ... Darwin did not account for the origin of variations; their forthcomingness was simply a datum for him." [17] Tennant is willing to grant that postulating a Designer to help explain what appears to be a design in nature is an inferential judgment, but he believes it is a reasonable inference, in any event, because in our experience what we call order is the result of an intentional agent or mind. If I come into a room and the chairs are completely disarranged—some backs are against the front, others are upside down while others are lying on their side—I probably would infer that the custodian has not been there and would undoubtedly proceed to arrange the chairs in an orderly fashion so that I could conduct a class. It might be argued that order exists in the eye of the beholder; in one sense that is true, but in another sense there is a conceptual design for some particular intended order. If someone does not perceive the order intended, steps can be taken to explain the intended order as it fulfills some functional purpose. I suppose it is possible to stand at the door of a room and toss chairs into a room for hundreds of thousands of times and, by chance, the chairs would all land in perfectly spaced rows facing the same way. The old argument that a hundred monkeys could sit at typewriters for billions of years and one of them, by chance, would type one of the works of Shakespeare stretches the boundaries of rationality for most of us to the edge. Lecomte du Noüy,[18] French scientist in this century, argues that it is mathematically improbable that the emergence of man, through a fortuitous evolutionary process, could occur.

The religious and particularly the theistic orientation to the physical universe portrays it as meaningful and more than a conglomeration of biochemical interactions without direction. This does not involve a completely determined system—as Whitehead clearly saw. A teleological world-view can be claimed within the framework of what we have called a "wider view," as affirming some unitive principle as operative within the whole. Michael Polanyi, Fellow of the Royal Society of London and Fellow of Merton College Oxford, examines the teleological problem in the light of our present scientific knowledge of living organisms and life itself. He cites the fact that when life originated on this planet several thousand million years ago it contained "long compounds of DNA," involving a linear sequence of four chemical radicals. "We think," he points out, "that the particular arrangement of these four chemical radicals conveys a vast system of notations, different for each kind of organism, which is transmitted chemically through successive generations ... [In addition] all members of the entire system of terrestrial living beings are carrying the same system of notations arranged in their own particular alignments. The entire complex of terrestrial life is based on chains of the same four DNA compounds, each organism having its own distinctive sequence of them." [19]

He outlines the very complicated process through which the DNA chain sustains the pattern of existing organisms and at the same time affords the opportunity for new Darwinian innovations to evolve into higher forms. Though we understand the chemical composition of the DNA, we are still faced with the question, "how the inanimate realm of the earth, from which all life has arisen, ever produced a sample of DNA compound." He adds, "A number of calculations estimating the probability that such a synthesis will take place accidentally have agreed in finding the chances of this so small, so rare, that the event appears virtually impossible." [20] He further addresses the problem of the transmission of life from one generation to the next and points out that "each step of the biological growth anticipates the subsequent step of growth by producing for its guidance a cellular body which will instruct the cellular

179

divisions of the next stage and will carry on the development to the final product." [21] This is a complex process in the development of the embryo that involves a timing of events at particular stages in the evolution of the organism. He claims that "no theory yet exists to explain how this can be done in a strictly chemical way," and suggests that these factors point to one of two conclusions:

> ... either the DNA is at once the blueprint and the builder (it is a sort of 'master molecule,' and it makes adaptations in some kind of purposeful way), or else it functions as merely another 'organ' in the body and so is interrelated in an immensely complicated way with every other organ (and *cell)* in adapting itself to the needs of that organism for growth and maintenance.[22]

It is interesting that molecular biologists speak of DNA functioning as a "code" for the physical and chemical development of the organism. Polanyi argues that "the base sequence in a DNA molecule is and must be extraneous to the chemical forces at work in the DNA molecule," [23] just as the manner in which a printed page is arranged is extraneous to the chemistry of the ink that is used. He acknowledges that how DNA functions could be the product of mere chance, but disagrees that such is the likely case. He concludes that some form "of gradient meaning is operative in evolution in addition to purely accidental mutation and plain natural selection and that this gradient somehow evokes ever more meaningful organizations (i.e. boundary conditions) of matter." [24] Thus he finds the teleological argument reasonable as long as it does not lead to a strict determinism.

It is not within the purview of science to resolve the *why* question and many scientists elect not to become philosophers, and particularly religious philosophers, because the evidence is not all in—and never will be—and there is much more work to be done that may alter the legitimacy of the extrapolations made by colleagues of a religious frame of mind and interest. Edmund Sinnott's attempt [25] to infer from the findings of the biological laboratory that there was evidence for "biological goal-seeking" as a property of the protoplasm, similar to human aspirations for intended goals, was met with less than general enthusiasm by his colleagues in biology. On the other hand, the only way we can deal with the problem of *why* things are as they are is to extrapolate from our experience and observations what might be the cause, particularly if we find reductionistic attempts at explanation inadequate. Teilhard de Chardin's work [26] is well known and has been well received by many people within the scientific community. He views the natural process as pointing toward an Omega point as it develops into higher and more meaningful forms. These are speculative interpretations of what the evolutionary process might mean, not proofs. They perform a heuristic function in challenging our minds to the possibility of greater than physical realms of meaning. The very intelligibility of the natural order may suggest that there is something about nature that makes it intelligible. Man, the minded-organism, is a product of nature. If mind be more than epiphenomenal and in some sense is ontologically real [27] there may be something about nature itself that bears the stamp of mind. The problem of the nature of the psyche is yet to be more adequately explored. In America we shy away from psychic phenomena because they are difficult to fit into the rigid stricture of a certain type of scientific methodology, while in England responsible psychical research is widely accepted. It would appear that if we are truly open to the spirit of the free investigation of phenomena we would be more willing to consider hypotheses that do not fit our limited criterion for truth. I have stressed this theme repeatedly—fully aware that the world is full of crackpot theories about the meaning of human existence; however, merely because this is true should not preclude serious thought about a wide range of possible interpretations of what constitutes reality.

The argument from design rests, in large part, upon the assumption that what is true of personal conscious experience is also true of nature. I refer specifically to the relationship of an agent to an intended action involving conscious awareness. This aspect of human experience constitutes one of the primary parts of what it means to be human. Man's capacity for self-conscious awareness and action is not shared by the lower animals. This can be debated, but it seems unlikely that the highest anthropomorphous ape is aware of his awareness, i.e. his I-ness. Yet man is very much aware that he is a person standing in relationship to other persons as a responsible agent. In fact, our whole moral system is predicated upon this assumption. My concern here is to examine briefly the interesting relationship between the agent and the act that he performs which may be analogically significant for our views of the universe within the framework of a wider teleological understanding.

The relationship between agent and action may serve as a model for conceiving God as agent within the world. For example, in throwing a baseball certain muscular movements are involved that can be studied scientifically and academicians in the field of physical education give a great deal of attention to what muscles are involved when a certain type of ball is thrown by a pitcher. However, the biochemical and muscular elements that are a part of the act of pitching a baseball do not determine whether it is a fast ball, curve ball or chargeup. What is intended by the pitcher makes all of the difference in the world. He may not place the ball in the position he intended or he may not throw the type of ball he would have liked, but his action as agent is the crucial fact. Or I may use many of the same muscles in the hand and forearm in posting a letter in a mailbox as in making a vulgar gesture, but the difference between the two acts is obvious: One serves the end of sending a letter to a friend and the other might produce a riot. John J. Compton analyzes the relationship between act and agent by examining the problem from a scientific or naturalistic and personalistic point of view. He finds the analogy of a human person, as an acting agent, fruitful in putting a conceptual handle on a comprehension of God's relationship to the world. As the agent functions within a bodily or physical frame of reference, so does God, as immanent purpose, operate within the world. At the same time, the agent, through the power of the mind, transcends his body to the extent that he determines to a large degree its function. Obviously all analogies are limited, but they do provide an intelligible framework for understanding aspects of the divine. Regarding this transcendent dimension, Compton says, "As with human agents, he [God] too transcends the particular behavioral expressions we see, with hidden, complex, and inclusive purposes of his own. The point is," he adds, "that the sense of God's personal transcendence, if we model it on the personal transcendence of the embodied, finite, and personal agent, does not require a radical dualism between God and the physical world." [28]

Parenthetically, I want to make it clear that the reflections made in the preceding statement on the argument from design are not intended as *proofs,* nor are they based on self-evident truths for which there is conclusive empirical evidence. Analogical reasoning does not consist of such empirical proofs; rather, it is an attempt to find conceptual models that are rooted in our experience of the world that might illumine a theistic understanding of God's relationship to the world. Gordon Kaufman states it well, "I am not claiming that the cosmic process provides *evidence* for believing in a God active through it; I am claiming merely that the evolutionary picture of nature and life currently painted in our scientific knowledge is not inconsistent with such a belief." [29]

The theistic portrayal of God's relationship to the natural order is not without serious problems. Earthquakes, tornadoes, epidemics and other natural disasters are grim realities and do great harm to a large number of people. Whether or not the arguments from a "wider teleological" perspective meet this problem is an open question. Many philosophical theologians suggest that if nature is viewed in its totality, a purposive view of nature can be sustained. Such generalities are of little comfort to a family which has lost their home because of a cyclone. Nonetheless, we are a part of a great ecosystem and cosmic process that, when viewed holistically, appears to be more ordered than chaotic. Man has not yet discovered how some disruptive elements within the larger order of things contribute to the whole. There appears to be a surd or irrational element within the cosmos. Within the biological order of the human body, we know that both the metabolic and catabolic process is going on. Our bodies are half-dead and half-alive as some tissues are building up and others are being destroyed. When we maintain this delicate balance within a bipolar biological process, we are healthy; and when the equilibrium is affected we are ill. Therefore to find a surd within nature does not destroy the possibility of a teleological world-view. Making God a part of the natural order implies that God limits Himself by the nature of the creative process itself. This is in contrast to a picture of God as omnipotent; if God is viewed as all-powerful and is absolutely omnipotent, then He can function in arbitrary ways. If on the other hand, God is viewed as freely self-limiting His function in accord with the laws of nature He has established, the arbitrary nature of deity is precluded.

The other way out of the dilemma is to affirm that God's ways are beyond human comprehension and accept His omnipotent relationship to man and the world on blind faith. For many of us, this requires a degree of credulity that threatens our attempt to understand, at least in part, God's relationship to the world in the light of what reason demands and in view of our deepest and most profound human experiences. The same problem arises when we speak of God's activity in history. If man is free, is God obligated to respect that freedom? If He is so morally bound, then He would freely limit himself to a non-violation of man's freedom. Most naturalistic theists view God in this way and thus run counter to the classical traditional orthodox picture of God as outlined in a previous section of this chapter.

But a more serious problem arises in a teleological understanding of nature's process and that is the second law of thermodynamics and the principle of entropy.

The "Big-Bang" theory affirms that several billion years ago all of the universe was in a single small volume. Then it began to explode and expand and has been doing so ever since. Countless galaxies of stars developed and planetary systems evolved. As the stars radiate their energy outward into intergalactic space, the density of energy in the universe will decrease and the time may come when no star will be able to provide life-sustaining light and warmth for any planet. But the time may also come when the force of the explosion is spent, and the universe collapses once more into a tiny volume—and starts all over again! In short, the universe as a whole, like the biological world, is evolving. Once it was young; now perhaps it is middle-aged; some day it will die.

Another theory is that the universe is in a "Steady-State." New units of matter and energy are continuously created in intergalactic space to replace those that have left. When old stars "die," new stars are "born." Hence, from this viewpoint, the universe has no beginning and has no end.[30]

This is a layman's version of the issue and scientists do not agree concerning this matter. "When you get to the size of the universe, the Second Law of Thermodynamics may or may not apply. We do not know." [31] We are speaking of possibilities covering billions of years; it is more likely that man will destroy himself by nuclear destruction than be destroyed by entropic forces within nature. In any event, the interrelationship between the order of physical nature, human life and consciousness is an experienced fact. The metaphysical problem is to find an adequate ontological ground for the unity of our experience. The theistic model we have briefly suggested is consonant with that experience.

Theism and Human Experience

Viktor E. Frankl, psychiatrist and philosopher, affirms throughout his writings [32] that the basic wellspring of human life is the "will-to-meaning"—a fundamental and innate desire in human consciousness to find a value or values that make life worth living. He came to this conclusion during his personal experience as a prisoner in several Nazi concentration camps and after observing how his fellow inmates tried to cope with the suffering and horror of their imprisonment. After the War he resumed his psychiatric teaching and practice in Vienna and developed a therapeutic technique known as "logotherapy," which attempts to help people find frames of reference for meaning that will assist them to live more fulfilled lives. Frankl does not develop his views into a full philosophical position, but

186

he does imply that the "will-to-meaning" is an aspect of man's nature and thus has ontological significance.

Tillich also points out that man is the only creature who is concerned with the problem of the meaning of his own being. Obviously, this is because he is a self-conscious agent and can reflect about his own being. In fact, without this capacity there would be no philosophy, religion, art, music, literature or any other personal attempt to make a "statement" about man and his world. Since we live in a predominantly activistic, sensate and non-reflective age [33] the larger ontological questions concerning the relationship of one's own being or existence to Being, in some religious or cosmic sense, are often placed on the back burner of our consciousness. The concern for meaning and "beingness" erupts at moments in our lives when such problems are inescapable and are forced upon us by the reality of our contingency when everything and everyone seem to fail us. At that moment, as we stand in our existential nakedness, does the force of the inner soul's search for meaning grasp our consciousness and becomes undeniable. As I have noted previously, these personal experiences may be moments of great ecstasy or great sorrow. Whichever they are, the symbolic power of their effect upon us points to the reality of our finitude as we seek a Source for meaning that leads beyond the temporal boundaries of our existence. Religious philosophers can provide no prescription or recipe that will cure the longing for cosmic identity and meaning. They can only suggest what the existential reality of man's inner quest may imply about the nature of man and the nature of the universe. To explain the universal phenomenon of man's search for an ontological ground for meaning as only the product of environmental and social factors, is to oversimplify the depth and significance of this phenomenon. There is no culture that has survived which has not developed some form of religion. Present day social experiments in thoroughly secularized societies, such as the USSR and China, are bound to fail because they are attempting to substitute finite experiences of meaning for those that are rooted in an "ultra-natural" dimension of existence. In my judgment, if these societies do survive, symbolic expressions of meaning will evolve that, by implication, have ontological meaning, and a new religion will develop that will attempt to relate man to the infinite. Granted, these forms of symbolic expression will be nontraditional and may be all for the good. I am suggesting, however, that if such societies are to survive they must, at least in some degree, meet man's ontic situation.

I want to examine four areas of human experience that seem to point in the direction of a theistic world-view on the one hand, and are illumined and clarified by a theistic world-view on the other hand. This statement may appear ambivalent and, in a sense it is, because I am not sure whether our world-view emerges primarily out of our primary experiences in the world or whether our world-view is essentially shaped by our language, the ways in which we are taught to think and other secondary-level experiences. In any event, the experiences that appear to me to have implications for a broader than naturalistic understanding of reality are: (1) Interpersonal experience; (2) Moral experience; (3) Aesthetic experience; and (4) Religious experience.

(1) Interpersonal Experience.

Man, by nature, is a social being. It is unlikely that Robinson Crusoe could have realized his highest human potential without finding Friday. In a very real sense, we are made for each other and in discovering each other we discover ourselves. This need is not fulfilled through casual social relationships in spite of the fact that most of our social ties are superficial. We often live and work in close geographical proximity to other persons, but have little sense of camaraderie or oneness. The relationship may involve a great deal of verbiage without any real communication; hence we often feel isolated and alone even though we are surrounded by others. In contrast, when persons *really* resonate, a spiritual quality emerges that defies reducibility to a single element—seemingly the whole person responds to another person at a level of the essence of each other's being—and both are changed. We call it love or deep friendship or give it some other appellation that conveys its abiding character. Unfortunately, we can never be certain of the authenticity of these kinds of experiences because of the complexity of all of the emotional, sensate and psychological factors involved. But as the sense of communion and oneness grows and is tested over periods of stress and difficulty, it soon becomes evident that it is no ephemeral experience but reaches to the very heart of the meaning of life and value. Many writers express this kind of experience as the "gift of love," that knows no limitations in its power and efficacy to bind and heal the human heart. It is no happenstance that when such love is expressed and freely given, it is said to mirror divine love that is without end.

I do not know when there has been a time in which there is so much talk about love and so little of it experienced as now. Since we are total human beings, the erotic aspects of love are always present. C. S. Lewis points this out in his book *The Four Loves* [34] where he distinguishes among affection, friendship, eros and charity. He suggests that there is no pure human love because of the dynamic structure of human personality that effects an intermingling of most of these elements. Of course, as a Christian he views charity or agape love as qualitatively the nearest to divine love. The term love has been so distorted by the tendency of our time to equate love with sex that it is difficult to remove that image from our minds, though we know full well that the deepest kinds of relationships may or may not involve physical or sensory aspects. The loyalties we cherish, the fraternal relationships that enrich our lives in so many ways, the new discoveries of mind and spirit that are made when a thought or experience is shared, or a loving act of concern for another human being without thought of return, are a part of the "gift of love."

There are two expressions of this quality of love that I find especially insightful—one by Viktor Frankl and the other by Erich Fromm:

> In love the beloved person is comprehended in his very essence, as the unique and singular being that he is; he is comprehended as a self, and as such is taken into another ego ... The person who is loved 'can't help' having the uniqueness and singularity of his self—that is, the value of his personality—realized. Love is not deserved, is unmerited—it is simply grace.[35]
>
> Love is the productive form of relatedness to others and to oneself. It implies responsibility, care, respect and knowledge, and the wish for the other person to grow and develop. It is the expression of intimacy between two human beings under the condition of the preservation of each other's integrity.[36]

Most secular humanists would applaud these statements as reflecting some of the most profoundly significant aspects of human experience and leave the matter there. But the question persists: Do such intersubjective experiences have any ontological significance? Do they point to a dimension of reality or being that is greater than their physical components? To suggest that, in the final analysis, human feeling and caring are a biochemical response to an external stim-

190

ulus in the form of a visual, sensory or imagined perception is reductionism to the level of absurdity. We write equations, not poetry, about biochemical properties. As is the case regarding so many issues I have been discussing, we could leave the problem at the point of the experience itself and the immediate meaning it provides for our lives, but for many of us this is not a satisfactory reply to the deeper question concerning the possible ontological significance of the experience. From a theistic point of view, interpersonal relationships bear an ontic quality that provides them a frame of conceptual reference for meaning which they would not otherwise have. If a person does not fit his experiences into a theistic world-view, the operational significance of intersubjective experiences is not necessarily lessened. However, the concern of this discourse is not on the practical effect such experiences have upon our lives, but rather the problem of a world-view that might provide them greater meaning from a holistic point of view.

At this point the writings of Gabriel Marcel are most pertinent. Marcel, well-known Roman Catholic philosopher, spoke of I and Thou relationships before these terms appeared in the writings of Martin Buber who made them a part of the theological and philosophical vocabulary of our time. Marcel's understanding of the meaning of a *presence* which is felt and experienced on the deepest level of human relationships is that such experiences are grounded in a *Presence,* or God. In order to clarify the meaning of *presence,* Marcel distinguishes between an *object* and a *presence.* He cites the common experience of being in a room with another person who is physically present but feels the *presence* of an individual several thousands of miles away as more real. In commenting on this type of experience, Marcel says, "One might say that what we have with this person, who is in the room, but somehow not really present to us, is communication without communion: unreal communication in a word." [37] In other words, the individual in the room did not make his *presence* felt. *Presence* involves intersubjectivity. An *object* can be transmitted; there is little about it that is ineffable. It can be described, defined or analyzed, but as an *object* it cannot be experienced. The way we relate to an *object* is qualitatively different from the manner in which we are grasped by a *presence*. It is this qualitative difference that provides a possible clue to the unique ontic character of the experience and points to the Divine Presence in which all true intersubjective communion participates. Marcel suggests that the deepest level of an interpersonal sense of presence can become the doorway to an appreciation for the mystery of Being as the divine within human life. Kenneth T. Gallagher summarizes this aspect of Marcel's thought when he says, "The more I love you, the surer I am of your eternity: the more I grow in authentic love for you, the deeper becomes my trust and faith in the Being which founds your being. There is no question of loving God or creature, since the more I really love the creature the more I am turned to the Presence which love lays bare." [38]

The similarities between the thought of Marcel and Buber are striking—both are concerned with the ontological meaning of human experience and believe that a clue to understanding the divine is through our deepest intersubjective experiences. Martin Buber, Jewish existentialist philosopher, is more widely known than Gabriel Marcel, and his writings have had a profound impact upon existential philosophic thought in our time. His early fascination with nature, his love of the theatre, his frequent visits to the Church of St. Thomas in Leipzig during his student days to listen to the music of Bach, and his Jewish background profoundly influenced his philosophy. For a time he was attracted to the Zionist movement but became disillusioned with its political aspects.[39] In his late twenties he became interested in Hasidism, a mystical movement that swept Eastern Jewry in the 18th and 19th centuries. The Hebrew word *Hasid* means pious and comes from the word *Hesed* which is translated as loving kindness or mercy. This was a movement of reaction against the traditional legalism of Jewish orthodoxy; its emphasis was upon piety, the love of God and neighbor. It also stressed the joy of God's creation and urged its followers to restore the original harmony that existed at creation between God and man.[40] The mystical emphasis made a deep impression on Buber and, according to his own testimony, the discovery of "the Hasidic soul" was "something indigenously Jewish (that) arose in me, blossoming, in the darkness of exile, to a new conscious expression. I perceived the very resemblance of man to God, as deed, as an act of becoming, as a duty." [41] Its emphasis upon a "yes" to life found a responsive place in Buber's heart. Though he broke with the formal aspects of Hasidic religious life and practice, there is little question that the mystical and pietistic element of its emphasis made an impact upon his writings and thought.

Briefly, Buber believes that the unity of life can best be found under the inspiration of eternal values—the Eternal Thou—that binds man to man beyond national boundaries and loyalties into a community of brotherhood. Man can only approach the eternal by becoming human in the most profound sense of the meaning of that term. The eternal, for Buber, is present in the now. When an I meets a Thou in interpersonal communication, which may or may not be verbal, a "between" evolves. For Buber, the "between" is ontologically *real* and is that binding force that unites men across all boundaries and is the infinite expressing its ultimate "Thouness" within the realm of the finite. The way to God is the path of human dialogue, encounter, relation and communion. At the close of Buber's "Prelude: Report on Two Talks," he cites the experience of having a long conversation with a friend who asked Buber to read some of his galley proofs to him. After Buber had read a number of pages, the man inquired, "How can you bring yourself to say 'God' time after time? ... What you mean by the name of God is something above all human grasp and comprehension, but in speaking about it you have lowered it to human conceptualization." [42] His friend further pointed out that the name 'God' has been used to justify the shedding of innocent blood and injustice. Buber replied, admitting that, in the name of 'God,' men have murdered one another and performed gross injustices; however, in the final analysis, "when all madness and delusion fall to dust, when they stand over against Him in the loneliest darkness and no longer say 'He, He' but rather sigh 'Thou,' shout 'Thou,' all of them on the one word, and when they add 'God,' is it not the real God of the children of man?" [43]

At the close of Buber's recounting this incident, he concludes, "For where two or three are *truly* together, they are together in the name of God." [44] (Italics mine.) I think these passages illustrate Buber's conception of God as both the ultimate Other or Thou as transcendent and also as the immanent *presence* when man meets in an I-Thou relationship. This is beautifully expressed when Buber says, "Of course, God is the 'wholly other'; but he is also the wholly same; the wholly present. Of course, he is the *mysterium tremendum* that appears and overwhelms; but he is also the mystery of the obvious that is closer to me than my own I." [45]

The Quaker movement within Protestantism has emphasized the immediacy of the Divine Presence within the life of the loving community. The Quakers or Friends, as they are also known, were a vital religious force within early American life and remain so to this day. Their weekly meetings of silence, in the spirit of reception and waiting, link the spiritual attunement and oneness of the group to the Divine Spirit. The force of this encounter cannot be understood until it is experienced, and it represents one of the deepest levels of communion and communication, in a non-verbal way, that many people have ever had. The Sunday Meeting at the Friends Meeting House in Cambridge, Massachusetts, is filled twice each Sunday morning as several hundred students and townspeople come to meditate in silence in each other's presence. But as both Marcel and Buber emphasize, this is no mere meeting of people in a close spatial and temporal relation; rather, it is a meeting of spirits within the *presence* of a universal spirit that unites them. I-Thou relationships, reflecting the presence of the divine, are not restricted to regular places or times, but can be realized when two hearts meet. From the theistic perspective, where there is this quality of communion, God is present. In these terms such experiences are sacred moments that elevate the human spirit above the expedient and selfish to the highest level of meaning and value.

(2) Moral Experience.

"Two things strike me with inexorable awe: The starry heavens above and the moral law within." Kant's famous dictum reflects a sense of the immediacy of the divine when one views the majesty and beauty of the universe and feels the urge within to a better and more noble life.

In striking contrast, the contemporary view, among some existentialist thinkers and shared by many secular humanists, is the notion that the universe is totally indifferent to man's search for meaning and values and that moral experience is the result of social necessity because without some freely accepted behavioral restraints and sense of duty, there could be no cohesive society. From this point of view, moral standards are derived from social sanctions that society establishes in order to assure its survival. Thus, it is further argued, when man realizes that social contracts involving obligations and a reciprocity of rights are in his own best interest, he will accept them as necessary for his own well-being. Therefore, there is nothing within the natural order that necessitates man becoming a valuing agent who distinguishes right from wrong and good from bad; such concerns are forced upon him by the nature of the social situation. Therefore, the ethical principles affirmed as necessary for the survival of the human race by *Humanist Manifesto II* are nothing more than reasonable moral social claims that will appeal to any rational agent who cares about the future of man on this planet. One could argue that their social necessity bears a kind of ontological character about them, but by and large these types of philosophical problems are viewed as irrelevant because they serve no functional purpose.

On the other hand, one might ask why societies are so structured that they warrant the establishment of normative ethical standards unless there is something about the nature of man himself that prods him to a higher level of fulfillment within a social context. Man, as both an individual and social being, is an essential part of nature so that the world cannot be described or explained as a whole without taking him into account as a valuing moral agent. If the evolutionary account of man is accurate, then both the intellectual and moral aspects of man's nature must be a part of nature's potency. Viewing man's moral capacity as a part of a larger cosmic whole places values within the nature of the purpose of life itself, and the same observations we noted earlier in our discussion of a purposive element within the natural order apply equally to man's moral concerns within the framework of his continuity with nature. F. R. Tennant expresses this wider teleological view when he says, "If man is Nature's child, Nature is the wonderful mother of such a child. Any account of her which ignores the fact of her maternity is scientifically partial and philo-sophically insignificant ... In the fulness of time Nature found self-utterance in a son possessed of the intelligent and moral status." [46] Or putting it differently, it is a kind of universe where the human potential for good can be real-ized in its individual and societal forms. The difference between this view and that of secular humanism is that this view places man's aspirations for the good and the better within the cosmic order of things in which man is a co-worker with the purposive ends that are a part of the natu-ral order which the theist calls God. Granted the theist does not escape the problems of relativism because he must interpret what values mean and how they are to be applied in concrete situations, but his attempt to find what the objective will of God might be for man tempers the kind of expediency of judgment that often plagues the relativist who finds no objective criterion for moral values and mean-ing possible.

An example of a naturalistic humanist attempt to escape the pitfalls of a complete relativism in moral values is Erich Fromm's understanding of those values that lead to human fulfillment and are, in some sense, a part of man's nature and arise out of fundamental human needs. These universal needs that stem from the condition of human existence are: (1) The need for relatedness, that is, the need to overcome separateness from other persons and from nature. (2) The need for transcendence, not in the religious sense of seeking a divine being who transcends nature, but the need to overcome one's creaturely status. Lower animals, Fromm contends, are shaped by their environments (they are auto-plastic), but man can create new environments out of exist-ing societal patterns and thus transcend the present and imagine the future (man is alloplastic). Transcendence is closely related to the need for creativity and self-determina-tion. (3) The need for rootedness or belonging. This involves the need for social ties that relate the individual to a larger social whole that includes both the present and the past. (4) The need for identity and a sense of personhood and individuality including a self-image of one's own uniqueness. (5) Finally, a need for a frame of orientation and devotion that will provide an individual with a sense of purpose and meaning—the need for a philosophy of life that will enable him to relate productively to himself and his world.[47]

Since these needs are a part of the given within man's nature, they bear an objective quality about them that man strives to fulfill and provide the outline for what is good for man. Fromm believes that man has an intuitive sense regarding his own functioning or dysfunctioning that tips the individual off, as it were, concerning that which will lead to his fulfillment or that which will destroy his fulfillment. Fromm calls this a "humanistic conscience," [48] and attributes this to an innate capacity that all men potentially have. I do not want to go further into Fromm's "empirical" basis for what constitutes the good life for man; I merely want to indicate one approach to the problem of normative values that stems from a secular world-view and does not end in complete relativism. The question remains, however, whether Fromm can justify his naturalistic ethic from his world-view that excludes a metaphysical or purposive element within nature itself which creates the conditions for the emergence of these distinctively human needs that imply how a person ought to live in order to be self-realized. It is interesting to note that all of these needs are essentially spiritual needs; Fromm, in contrast to Abraham Maslow,[49] does not mention physical or survival needs as fundamental to personal fulfillment.

If man's *essential* nature is expressed in the givenness of certain universal needs, then it would appear that some ontological basis for values is implied. I believe the reason many Roman Catholic students find Fromm's writings fruitful is because they sense in them an equivalent to a "natural law" ethical philosophy that is made explicit in the ethics of St. Thomas. Fromm might not appreciate this tie of his own thought to a "natural law" ethic, but I think his views imply a metaphysical position he does not make explicit. Walter A. Weisskopf makes a helpful distinction between the concrete, actual historical conditions which determine the content of values and the ultimate ground of values. While the content of values is relative to societies and cultures, values also have an ontological source. He adds this comment, "Even those who reject metaphysical arguments can learn from history that all cultures derived their ultimate values from a basic concept or symbol which stood for the ground of being, such as God, nature, the universe, etc. Wherever the relation of this awareness between the ground of being and values was lost, values began to disintegrate." [50]

These observations do not justify in any conclusive way the theistic position about man as a valuing agent and God as the source or ground of all values, but I do think they are provocative. A. C. Garnett, professor of philosophy for many years at the University of Wisconsin, views the natural tendency of man's "feeling-striving process" which strives "creatively to realize larger and larger possibilities of good wherever they may be found" [51] to the activity of God as the immanent good within the life of mankind. The theistic perspective places the search of man for higher values within a cosmic frame of reference of meaning and sees the teleological process at work within the moral sensibilities of man as well as operative within the natural physical order.

No discussion of theism and moral experience is complete without reference to Immanuel Kant's classic work and thought regarding this problem. I began this section of the essay by reference to Kant and will end this discussion referring back to him. Kant was convinced that God's existence could not be established by pure reason; yet he found that the compelling force of the divine within human experience needed explanation. Where could it be found? Hume's skepticism had profoundly influenced Kant's thought to the extent that Kant affirmed the *noumenon* or "Thing-in-itself" could never be known. If that be true, then on what basis, he asked, can I affirm moral or religious truth at all? He found his "answer" in the immediacy of moral experience or "practical reason" as the ground for religious belief. In contrast to the rationalists who depended upon pure theoretical reason to justify their beliefs, and in contrast to the pietists who rooted their faith upon a personal and special type of religious experience, Kant predicated his case for the legitimacy and necessity of religious faith upon the nature of duty. He saw the sense of obligation or duty that all men sense as qualitatively different from other types of experience. He saw it as an "inexplicable fact of experience" in contrast to sensate or affective experiences including desire and impulse. He further believed that it falls outside the realm of normal causal relations within a temporal order and viewed it as a part of one's being as a rational agent that implies the existence of a self that is more real than the external world. Assuming that moral experience, so described, cannot be adequately explained by external social causes, the question arises: From whence does it come?

At this point he does not speak dogmatically but affirms as "reasonable beliefs" or postulates certain beliefs as necessary in order to give adequate meaning to the intuitively sensed and persistent moral claim upon life. These postulates are: (1) The freedom of the self to discharge its duty because if we do not assume we can do what the moral law demands, the moral law has no meaning. In other words, "ought implies can." (2) The immortality of the soul as a condition of future existence in which all of the moral law's demands can be met. It is obvious that in this life one cannot fulfill completely his highest duty; he can only approximate it. Therefore, if it be a moral universe, Kant argued, there must be the possibility for the realization of the *summum bonum* and infinite progress toward full realization of the moral law; otherwise the sense of moral obligation would end only in frustration. In other words, immortality is necessary to the fulfillment of obligation. (3) The existence of God as the highest Good, one who actualizes in himself all of the attributes of absolute goodness, and assures that the *summum bonum* is possible. The heart of religion is "to recognize one's duties as divine commands."

In Kant's extensive private notes discovered after his death, he suggested that the idea of God was not merely a "trans-subjective Being" but was "immanent in the human spirit." From this perspective "God is the morally practical self-legislative Reason." To say there is a God is to suggest that there is "in the human morally self-determining Reason a highest principle which determines itself, and finds itself compelled unremittingly to act in accordance with such a principle." [52]

There is no question that the voice of conscience is a strong voice and that man, as distinquished from other creatures, is consciously aware of the meaning of such terms as "obligation" and "duty" and can attempt to give expression to these claims upon his life. Kant placed definitional parameters around the term "duty," and did not leave it to the relativity of societies and cultures to determine—his three formulations of the categorical imperative are important parts of his ethical philosophy.[53] The point I am making is that Kant provided a conceptual framework for moral experience that is consonant with a theistic world-view and provokes modern man to consider the adequacy of a purely naturalistic view of the moral life. Here again, it seems to me, the nature of the immediacy of moral experience points to something both within ourselves and outside of ourselves that urges us on to something better for mankind as we attempt to achieve a higher good and, at the same time, a theistic world-view places this experience within an ontological framework that gives it moment and urgency.

(3) Aesthetic Experience.

One of the most universally felt experiences of man is the aesthetic sense expressing itself through a wide variety of literary and artistic forms—including scientific and technical models—which become the media for the language of the soul. It is curious that an experience that is primarily rooted in the senses and apprehended by them bears a spiritual quality so unlike a purely sensuous experience. This, in part, explains the artificiality of a mind/body dichotomy because an aesthetic experience involves the total person as he is enveloped and becomes one with that which is being experienced. I think it is this aspect of Zen Buddhism's [54] appreciation and understanding of the experience of beauty as a primary, intuitive, pre-cognitive sense of immediacy and needs no explanation that is very close to the mystical experience of the divine. From the Zen point of view, beauty is! It is to be experienced, entered into, enjoyed and expressed. Thus one cannot teach beauty or convey beauty —it simply exists! If you ask a Zen Master by what criteria he determines what is beautiful, he would find the question, not only irrelevant, but amusing.

A number of years ago I was lecturing to a group of public school teachers in the lovely San Jacinto Mountain area near Los Angeles about the Zen teaching regarding the need to transcend the subject/object dichotomy so characteristic of the western approach to phenomena. I was applying this insight to the beauties of nature. Suddenly I realized that we were in the mountains among beautiful trees and landscapes, so I stopped talking and suggested that we let the trees speak to us as we sat silently in their presence. Thus for a few minutes we said nothing and in the silence of the moment experienced the beauties around us in a direct and immediate way. One of the reasons western man shuts himself off from aesthetic experience is because he is so prone to put everything into words, to classify, or define what he is experiencing that he loses the reality of the experience he is attempting to grasp. The experience of beauty is an immediate intuition, the response of an aesthetic sentiment to what is felt and observed. The individual knows it when he sees it—it may not be the eye of the body, but as Plato understood true perception, it is seen by the "eye of the soul."

In addition to the naturalness as well as givenness of the aesthetic response, there is a close relationship between the aesthetic and the ethical. Plato placed Truth, Beauty and Goodness at the pinnacle of his metaphysics. His conviction that there is a natural relationship between beauty and goodness permeates his writings. It was inconceivable to him that a good man, who integrated the appetitive, spirited and rational parts of his soul into a unified whole, would not also have an appreciation for truth and beauty. In fact, Plato's system of education, outlined in *The Republic,* stressed the necessity for children to have early experiences of beauty, harmony and rhythm. He assumed that the quality of art, poetry and music children experienced was directly related to the kind of ethical life they would later lead. He was convinced that "ugliness and discord and inharmonious motion are nearly allied to ill words and ill nature, as grace and harmony are the twin sisters of goodness and virtue and bear their likeness." [55] Plato believed that evil was the result of ignorance because, if one caught a glimpse of Truth, Beauty and Goodness, then falsehood, ugliness or evil would never be a viable option for his life. Though one would not want to defend Plato's views on this point in a literal way, nonetheless there is a compelling quality about aesthetic, moral and religious experience that reaches the depth of one's own being and leaves one never the same.

In the language of our day we speak of a "beautiful person" as referring to a quality of a person's character or essential being. Or we observe an act of kindness or caring and call it "beautiful." Such descriptions of behavior and character can become trite and meaningless, but they can also be expressive of an inner beauty an individual exhibits that permeates, what may be, a frail and unattractive body. All of us have seen elderly people who are in failing health and whose physical beauty has been destroyed by sickness and disease but who, nevertheless, have retained a quality of spirit that is indeed beautiful. The interface between the beautiful and the good—the aesthetic sense and the moral sense—has been viewed as self-evident by many thinkers in the western tradition. In more recent times, the Earl of Shaftsbury, Francis Hutcheson and Friedrich Schiller—all of the 18th century—saw clearly the kinship of the good and the beautiful.

One of the greatest sources for aesthetic experience has been the beauty and order of nature which have struck men with responses of awe and reverence since the beginning of conscious awareness. It is no happenstance that early man thought of the heavens as the place of the gods and identified astral bodies with divinities. Thus the interrelationship between the religious and aesthetic experience is clearly seen throughout history. The beauty, harmony, order, symmetry, unity, perfection and movement of the spheres have placed aesthetic experience in a direct relationship to a world ground that gives meaning to the universe. In these terms, the universe becomes a beautiful work of art. Pantheistic expressions of nature's beauties are expressed throughout western history. From Cleanthes' *Hymn to Zeus* to the poetry of William Wordsworth, as well as the many passages in the Bible to the glories and beauties of nature, man's feeling for the divine has been inextricably tied to aesthetic experience.

There is a curious admixture of these two elements in the thought of Marsilio Ficino, a transition figure between the Medieval and Renaissance periods, who was a Platonic and Neo-Platonic scholar. He saw the universe as a sublime world-unity and believed that man, through the power of his soul, could find this unity as he moves into higher and higher degrees of insight and love toward God. His stress upon man's dignity places him within a Renaissance frame of reference and his emphasis upon unity with God relates him to the medieval world-view. The Neo-Platonic perspective, mentioned in an earlier chapter, provides for him a framework for the union of the aesthetic and the religious.

The manifold expressions in religiously motivated artistic, musical and literary forms are too numerous to mention. Though the motivation for building many of the great cathedrals of Europe was prompted by political and other mundane factors, their architectural forms are expressive of the human spirit's outreach toward the divine. These magnificent structures with their stained glass windows and other forms of art are monuments to man's search for ways of expressing the inexpressible. To suggest that these forms of creative talent, in the richness of their symbolic meaning, are merely a projection of a restless soul's search for beauty and truth in a value-less universe without objective validity, is to reduce them to a subjective level of expression that fails to acknowledge the possibility that they are rooted and grounded in an ontological dimension of meaning.

It seems to me that a theistic world-view provides a conceptual frame of reference which clarifies and enriches the meaning that these human acts of creativity deserve. The immanent character of the divine is seen within the beautiful aspects of nature and within man's capacity for creativity in the artistic forms he develops. As Peter Bertocci observes, man continues to build and create "cathedrals and symphonies, epic poems, sonnets, and lyrics, sculptures and paintings. And these abilities," he adds, "bear witness to a life within them nurtured and inspired by the very processes which constitute their being." [56] John Elof Boodin, who saw both man and nature as mind-directed, gives a theistic interpretation to aesthetic activity as a form of spiritual creativeness when he says,

> It is for us ... most reasonable to believe that the genius of nature works as an artist; that the artistic creativeness of man is the outcome of this activity; and that our insight into nature is made possible by the creative empathy between the creative mind of the universe.[57]

(4) Religious Experience.

This is the bottom line for one who believes in a theistic world-view. His experience of the divine may include the aesthetic, moral and interpersonal aspects of life, but in the final analysis unless one has had a personal encounter with the divine in some primary and immediate way, the question of God's existence remains a problem. Most people who call themselves religious have had experiences within a socially identified religious context, but too few have had a personal encounter with the divine that they can call their own. The same is true of many other experiences within institutional structures. A student may attend four years of college and even reach graduate school and never have an experience *of* learning that engages his entire being and "turns him on" to knowledge. An authentic religious experience carries with it a quality of its own confirmation—a new world is discovered, new insights are gained and a level of awareness is reached that was never dreamed possible. The impact that a higher level of religious consciousness has made upon many of the youth in our time is a phenomenon that is not to be taken lightly and, without question, has been a transforming force in the lives of many individuals. Most of the great visionaries of the past were called mad because they challenged the status quo and saw truth from a different perspective than others in their society. Of course there are a great many dangers in a self-authenticating experience because they often lead to extremism and fanaticism that knows no rational boundaries. However, the history of religion is replete with accounts of men and women who have found a spiritual center for their lives through their tradition. When religious experience is rooted within the richness of the person's own tradition which bears the witness of the ages, it is unlikely to be extreme or fanatical, but grounded in the ontological verities which the tradition symbolizes through its rites and ceremonies. For many people, nonetheless, the rituals and traditions become a substitute for that which they represent and as the result they become meaningless and repetitious. Perhaps in the habitual pattern of observing the Holy Days and other ceremonies, the individual will catch an occasional glimpse of what they mean and why they have been established, but unless he enters into the richness of these symbolic forms as a participant, and not merely as an observer, they will become lifeless in his hands. The attempt to recapture the essence of a religious tradition in all of its vitality and original power is what gives rise to reformation movements. It is paradoxical that within a short time, the reformation needs to be reformed in order to give vitality to that which aroused it originally. Form without content or substance is deadly, and nothing defeats the ongoing power of a movement more than its spiritual obsolescence. If personal religious experience is the bottom line, as I have suggested, then why is it necessary to give the experience of the divine cognitive meaning and structure in the form of a theology or religious philosophy? Why not take the Zen Buddhist posture that all attempts to elucidate primary experience are futile? Or why not take the position held by many others that God reveals himself to man in ways that are ineffable and beyond human understanding because the truth of the experience is accepted on faith without the need for further intellectual examination or explanation?

If one wants to take either of these points of view, he has every right to do so, but on the other side of the coin there is the issue of the intellectual aspect of man's nature that wants reasonable answers to questions—the spirit of the inquiring mind that presses for further understanding. I would agree that, in the final analysis, the religious encounter is personal and ineffable and breaks the boundaries of rationality, but to divorce it completely from other aspects of our experience as we attempt to relate it in some coherent way to what we think we know in and through ordinary experience, is to be unfaithful to the legitimacy of intellectual inquiry which presses for a more complete comprehension of what is affirmed. This is particularly true of educated people who want to consider the intellectual viability of a claim before entering into it with their whole selves. And, in my judgment, this is a legitimate concern. It seems to me that a theistic world-view that includes as a part of its components the validity of moral, religious and intersubjective experience as integral to developing a comprehensively adequate religious philosophy is justified.

I do not want to raise the whole faith/reason controversy

concerning which precedes the other. In a sense the disposition for faith is a prerequisite for religious experience; yet, on the other hand, the soil can be prepared for faith by the interaction between faith and doubt. In reality, the response of faith and the vitality of religious awareness is the product of many factors similar to those we discussed in the development of a world-view. *As it is difficult to learn to swim without getting into the water, it is hard to be profoundly moved religiously unless one places himself in the kind of "environment" that will facilitate an openness to the divine.* I have used the word environment in a very special sense because the total "environment" in which we live includes attitudes and many other subjective elements, as well as the external world of which we are a part. Both the internal and external environments condition our responses. The divine spirit, whatever it is, does not operate within a vacuum.

However, there is a broader link than the individual relationship to the divine and that is the spiritual tie that binds men and women of faith within a world community of faith that is broader than sectarian religious lines. There is an increasing interest among men and women everywhere in this type of spiritual universalism that endeavors to understand the religious impulse from a broader culturally-determined spiritual perspective. It is a curious fact that religion has been such a divisive force in the life of men when it claims to be grounded in an omnipresent reality that transcends all national and racial boundaries. Although it takes mankind a long time to see his own religion in this perspective, there are some signs that man is coming of age and is beginning to reach out across the artificial parameters of his own tradition. This is not to suggest that one can put all of the good from all of the religions of the world into a religious mixmaster and bring about a concoction called "religion." For most of us in the

West certain forms of Buddhism are not live emotional options; we are too conditioned to western ways of thinking, living and feeling. But that does not mean that we cannot find a common spiritual bond that unites us and is rooted in our finite/infinite natures. People linked by a common spiritual consciousness can be one and at the same time retain their own symbolic forms of expression which provide a special kind of meaning. The writings of William Ernest Hocking on this point are most fruitful.[58]

The major difference between the naturalistic humanist and the theist is at this point. Naturalism insists on limiting reality to man and nature which may or may not have some ontological or spiritual ground we have been describing. But to interpret the well-nigh universality of the religious response to the universe as an epiphenomenal expression of a subjective side of man's nature does not seem adequate to explain its pervasiveness and value.

The late Thomas Merton is one of the most inspiring figures of our time. Son of parents that were both artists, deeply sensitive to nature and religious art, student of language and literature, and a college professor of literature, Merton became a Trappist monk at the age of twenty-six. He is best known for his book, *The Seven Storey Mountain* and is only now becoming widely known for his attempt to build spiritual bridges between western and eastern religious traditions. He was a prolific writer and though he was in a strict order that practiced a great deal of solitary prayer and meditation, he conducted a lively correspondence with monks in India and other parts of the world. In 1968 he was given permission by his Order to visit Asia where he met with monks in various parts of the eastern world in an attempt to find that Spiritual Center or Source they shared in common. Tragically he died an untimely death in Bangkok, but he left behind the notes and papers he had prepared on the trip that give us some insight into his feelings about the common aspects of the spiritual life. Two observations are of particular relevance to this discussion: (1) A common preoccupation with the "radical inner depth of one's religious philosophical beliefs, the inner experimental 'ground' of those beliefs," and (2) "a special concern for inner transformation, a deepening of consciousness toward an eventual breakthrough and discovery of a transcendent dimension of life beyond that of the ordinary empirical self and of ethical and pious observance." [59]

Though Merton is speaking of monastic experience primarily, I believe that at the heart of his description, to a lesser degree perhaps, is the root of what constitutes lived-through experience of the divine. The question of where such experiences fit into a world-view is of crucial importance. From the standpoint of a complete naturalism, mystical experiences have no other than human and natural points of reference; many mystical humanists, such as W. T. Stace and others, settle the matter on this level. For the theist, however, the transcendent dimension, as the Ultimate Ground and Source for religious experience as expressed within the life of man and nature, completes a picture with a degree of objectivity that a thoroughgoing naturalism fails to provide. Men and women throughout the ages, in their living response to life as experienced on the most primary and elementary levels, have discovered in these experiences a sense of *Presence* about which Marcel so effectively writes. The problem in an encapsulated age that binds us to itself in so many ways, is to unstop our ears, open our eyes, so that we can hear and see and experience the divine in our midst. If we do this, then the sense of *presence* we discover through a life of dialogue with others and with nature may unlock for us the meaning of *Presence* or God.

There are many problems a theistic world-view does not resolve. It could be an "illusion" á la Freud; it could be an attempt to compensate for the reality of tragedies we cannot face; it might be the result of a social conditioning process that has brainwashed us to the point that we cannot view reality in any other way. Finitude limits us to psychological certitude. It is a faith, however, that many men and women find existentially and conceptually meaningful. As we have noted, one's world-view is not arrived at solely as the result of empirical or rational demonstration. Ultimately the adequacy or inadequacy of whatever faith we live by is tested on the anvil of our experience. In this essay, we have only attempted to present the broad outlines of a naturalistic and theistic world-view and make some observations about them. We are all products of our time; the clock cannot be turned back to the psychological comfort that a pre-Copernican cosmology afforded us. We live in a post-Copernican, post-Darwinian and post-Freudian age. However, it is my conviction that a theistic world-view I have tried to explicate is consistent with what we think we know scientifically about our world and ourselves, going beyond the naturalistic assumptions underlying scientific investigation, to illumine and enrich our experience. C. A. Coulson, formerly Rouse Ball Professor of Applied Mathematics at Oxford University, rejecting the science/religion dichotomy, states a possible union between them when he says, "If we cannot bring God in at the end of science, He must be there at the very start, and right through it. We have done wrong to set up any sharp antithesis between science and religion... There is no other way out of our impasse than to assert that science is one aspect of God's presence, and scientists therefore part of the company of His heralds." [60]

One concluding word: Fortunately most of us, as human beings, are better than the limited interpretations we put on our experience. The common humanity we share links men and women of honest intent and purpose in the search for truth. Whatever our world-views might be, may we be honorable persons living our lives with integrity and openness—openness to each other and to that Ground and Source of Being called by countless Names.

ADDENDUM

Special Closing Prayer
(Offered at the First Spiritual Summit Conference
in Calcutta by Father Thomas Merton)

I will ask you to stand and all join hands in a little while. But first, we realize that we are going to have to create a new language of prayer. And this new language of prayer has to come out of something which transcends all our traditions, and comes out of the immediacy of love. We have to part now, aware of the love that unites us, the love that unites us in spite of real differences, real emotional friction . . . The things that are on the surface are nothing, what is deep is the Real. We are creatures of love. Let us therefore join hands, as we did before, and I will try to say something that comes out of the depths of our hearts. I ask you to concentrate on the love that is in you, that is in us all. I have no idea what I am going to say. I am going to be silent a minute, and then I will say something. . . .

Oh God, we are one with You. You have made us one with You. You have taught us that if we are open to one another, You dwell in us. Help us to preserve this openness and to fight for it with all our hearts. Help us to realize that there can be no understanding where there is mutual rejection. Oh God, in accepting one another wholeheartedly, fully, completely, we accept You, and we thank You, and we adore You, and

213

we love You with our whole being, because our being is in Your being, our spirit is rooted in Your spirit. Fill us then with love, and let us be bound together with love as we go our diverse ways, united in this one spirit which makes You present in the world, and which makes You witness to the ultimate reality that is love. Love has overcome. Love is victorious. Amen.[61]

NOTES

1. I found Gordon Kaufman's *God the Problem.* (Cambridge: Harvard University Press, 1972) particularly insightful, especially Chapter 9, "Secular, Religious, and Theistic World-Views."
2. A philosophical principle characteristic of most American's belief appears in a cassette tape, "Zuckerkandlism," by Robert Hutchins. Available at the Center for the Study of Democratic Institutions.
3. Oesterley-Robinson, *Hebrew Religion: Its Origin and Development.* (London: SPCK, 1947, Second and Revised Edition). See particularly Part I, "The Background," on the remnants of primitive religious beliefs in early Hebrew religion, pp. 3-125.
4. The *Timaeus,* 27c ff.
5. The problem of categorizing current religious thought is illustrated in John Macquarrie's *Twentieth Century Religious Thought* (N.Y.: Harper and Row, 1963) division of contemporary religious thought under nineteen different movements. Since the publication of this volume, the "death of God" movement, radical theology and the theology of hope have been influential forces. Perhaps the most serious omission from my four theistic perspectives is the existentialist movement, but it seems to me that this posture has influenced pro-

foundly all of the points of view I have cited, and particularly figures such as Paul Tillich and others, who do not fit into any of the religious categories mentioned. Therefore, when I mention names in the Notes to be identified with these divisions, it should be understood that these persons are, in many cases, loosely placed within the theological rubric being discussed.

6. The major figures in the history of western theology held to the basic position I have outlined. The key issue centers upon the conception of God's relationship to the natural order and the 'abrogation' of 'natural law' through God's omnipotent will and power. Two widely read contemporary supernaturalists are: C. S. Lewis, *God in the Dock: Essays in Theology and Ethics.* (Grand Rapids: Wm. Eerdman's Pub. Co., 1970); *Miracles.* (N.Y.: The Macmillan Co., 1947) and E. L. Mascall, *Christian Theology and Natural Science.* (N.Y.: The Ronald Press, 1956).

7. Evangelical writers are showing greater theological and philosophical sophistication than ever before. Some of the leading writers are: Norman L. Geisler, *Philosophy of Religion.* (Grand Rapids: Zondervon Pub. Co., 1974); J. I. Packer, *'Fundamentalism' and the Word of God.* (Grand Rapids: Wm. Eerdmans, 1958); Carl F. Henry, Ed., *Basic Christian Doctrines.* (N.Y.: Holt, Rinehart and Winston, 1963) Wilson-Womack, Ed., *Pillars of Faith.* (Grand Rapids: Baker Book House, 1973); John W. Montgomery, *The Suicide of Christian Theology.* (Minneapolis: Bethany Fellowship, Inc., 1970).

8. It is difficult to find established and recognized scholars who will identify themselves as "fundamentalist." Yet, the religious programs on radio and television are predominantly "fundamentalistic" in theology. Many of

these groups are not aligned with any established denomination and call themselves non-denominational. They seldom use the term "ecumenical." They seek, by and large, to find their roots in apostolic Christianity. Protestant groups in the south, who are "fundamentalist," are found throughout the mainline churches, but often their clergy are more liberally inclined than the laity, particularly if the denomination holds to graduate training as a requirement for ordination. Unaccredited Bible schools, institutes and similar schools prepare the ministry for a great many of these independent groups. Educational qualifications vary within Protestant denominations, but most of the major churches require three years training in theology and related subjects beyond the A.B. degree. Tracts, pamphlets and booklets dominate "fundamentalist" publications.

9. See Shirley Jackson Case, *Experience with the Supernatural in Early Christian Times*. (N.Y. : The Century Press, 1922) for illustrations of stories about supernatural events in movements contemporary with the early Christian period.

10. Classic neo-orthodox positions on the Continent were stated in the writings of Karl Barth and Emil Brunner and in this country Reinhold Niebuhr's two volume work, *The Nature and Destiny of Man*. (N.Y.: Charles Scribner's Sons, 1941 and 1943) had a profound effect upon American theological thought. As a philosophical statement, John Hick's *Faith and Knowledge*. (Ithaca: Cornell University Press, 1957) and his *Philosophy of Religion*. (Englewood Cliffs: Prentice-Hall, 1963) provide an excellent summary. Roman Catholic statements that stand on the mid-ground between orthodoxy and existentialism are Leslie Dewart's, *The Future*

216

of Unbelief. (N.Y.: Herder and Herder, 1966). Also, Hans Küng, *On Being a Christian,* tr. by Edward Quinn. (Garden City: Doubleday and Co., 1966) represents a liberal Roman Catholic point of view.

11. In this section, I am not interested primarily in the social gospel aspects of the liberal theological movement in Protestantism. Rather, my focus is on the development of a natural theology that identifies God's activity within the natural evolutionary process as a purposive principle directed toward ends that contribute to human well-being, in contrast to the view that nature is a blind force without direction. The philosophers and theologians representing this point of view are legion. I will mention only a few: John Elof Boodin, *God.* (N.Y.: The Macmillan Co., 1934), *God and Creation.* (N.Y.: The Macmillian Co., 1934); Henri Bergson, *Creative Evolution,* tr. by Arthur Mitchell. (N.Y.: The Modern Library, 1911); Alfred North Whitehead, *Process and Reality.* (N.Y.: The Macmillan Co., 1929); Henry Nelson Wieman, *Man's Ultimate Commitment.* (Carbondale: So. Illinois Press, 1958); Charles Hartshorne, *A Natural Theology for Our Time.* (La Salle: Open Court, 1967); F. R. Tennant, *Philosophical Theology,* 2 vols. (Cambridge: At the University Press, 1935); Teilhard de Chardin, *The Phenomenon of Man.* (N.Y.: Harper and Row, 1961); John B. Cobb, *A Christian Natural Theology.* (Phila: The Westminster Press, 1965). By and large these writers share an "empirical" orientation to theological questions. A good summary of empirical philosophies of religion is James A. Martin, Jr., *Empirical Philosophies of Religion.* (Morningside Heights: Kings Crown Press, 1945).

12. See J.F.T. Bugental's essay, "The Challenge That Is

Man," in Bugental (Ed.), *The Challenges of Humanistic Psychology.* (N.Y.: McGraw-Hill Book Company, 1967), pp. 5-11.

13. Bertocci is here writing in the name of Edgar S. Brightman. He has skillfully edited many of Brightman's writings into a coherent and readable single volume. *Person and Reality* (N.Y.: The Ronald Press, 1958), p. 335.

14. Harlow Shapley, *Beyond the Observatory.* (N.Y.: Charles Scribner's Sons, 1967), p. 16.

15. Thomas Aquinas, *Summa Theologica,* I, 3. *Basic Writings of St. Thomas Aquinas.* Ed., A.C. Pegis 2 vols.; (N.Y.: Random House, 1945), I, p. 22.

16. Frederick Ferre's edited volume of William Paley's *Natural Theology.* (Selections) (Indianapolis: Bobbs-Merrill Co., Ind., 1963). The "Introduction" is an excellent summary of Paley's arguments. Also, Ferre's, *Basic Modern Philosophy of Religion.* (N.Y.: Charles Scribner's Sons, 1967), Chapter 5, pp. 149 ff. on Paley is helpful.

17. F. R. Tennant, *Philosophical Theology.* (Cambridge: At the University Press, 1937), II, p. 85.

18. Lecomte du Noüy, *Human Destiny.* (N.Y.: Longmans, Green and Co., 1947).

19. Michael Polanyi and Harry Prosch, *Meaning.* (Chicago: The University of Chicago Press, 1975), p. 164. This book is essentially Polanyi's, but written and edited with the assistance of his former student, Harry Prosch.

20. *Ibid.,* p. 165. Most mathematicians would question the scientific validity of such after-the-fact analyses.

21. *Ibid.,* pp. 165, 166.

22. *Ibid.,* p. 167.

23. *Ibid.,* p. 172.

24. *Ibid.*, p. 173.
25. Edmund W. Sinnott, *The Biology of the Spirit.* (N.Y.: The Viking Press, 1955). For many years, Prof. Sinnott was a natural scientist at Yale University.
26. Particularly Teilhard de Chardin's *The Phenomenon of Man.* (N.Y.: Harper and Row, 1959).
27. One of the best books I have read recently on the mind-body problem is: H. Tristram Englehardt, Jr., *Mind-Body: A Categorical Relation.* (The Hague: Marinus Nijhoff, 1973), in which he argues for the ontic significance of both mind and body and rejects a monism that would reduce one to the other.
28. John J. Compton, "Science and God's Action in Nature," in Ian G. Barbour, Ed. *Earth Might Be Fair.* (Englewood Cliffs: Prentice-Hall Inc., 1972), pp. 39, 40. I found this essay particularly suggestive. Compton's views are similar to those of John C. Cobb as expressed in his *A Christian Natural Theology* (Phila: Westminster Press, 1965) and Gordon D. Kaufman's *God the Problem,* cited earlier.
29. Gordon D. Kaufman, *op. cit.,* p. 139.
30. Kirtley Mather, "Creation and Evolution," in Harlow Shapley, *Science Ponders Religion,* (N.Y.: Appleton-Century-Crofts Inc., 1960), pp. 32 ff. Shapley identifies Georges Lemaitre and George Gamow with the "Big Bang" theory and Herman Bondi, Thomas Gold, and Fred Hoyle with the "Steady-State" hypothesis. *Beyond the Observatory, op. cit.,* pp. 27, 28.
31. In conversation with Gibson Reaves, Professor of Astronomy, University of Southern California. I am deeply indebted to him for his clear explanation of these and many other scientific matters.
32. Viktor E. Frankl, *From Death-Camp to Existentialism.* (Boston: Beacon Press, 1959) and later appearing in a

revised edition, *Man's Search for Meaning.* Also, see Frankl's *The Doctor and the Soul.* (New York: Alfred A. Knopf, 1960).

33. P.A. Sorokin's *The Crisis of Our Age.* (N.Y.: E.P. Dutton and Company, 1941) is an excellent statement on this theme, particularly his discussion of "The Crisis of the Contemporary Sensate System of Truth," pp. 116 ff.

34. C. S. Lewis, *The Four Loves.* (N.Y.: Harcourt, Brace and World, Inc., 1960).

35. *Viktor Frankl, op. cit., The Doctor and the Soul.* pp. 149, 150.

36. Erich Fromm, *Man for Himself.* (Greenwich, Conn.: Fawcett Publications, Inc., 1970).

37. Gabriel Marcel, *The Mystery of Being,* I. "Reflection and Mystery," (Chicago: Henry Regnery Co., 1960), p. 252.

38. Kenneth T. Gallagher, *The Philosophy of Gabriel Marcel.* (N.Y.: Fordham University Press, 1962), p. 80.

39. Aubrey Hodes' book, *Martin Buber: An Intimate Portrait* (N.Y.: The Viking Press, 1971) is an excellent biographical and anecdotal source for an insight into Buber's life and thought.

40. For a good summary of the influence of Hasidism and mystical thought on Buber's philosophy, see Maurice Friedman, *Martin Buber: The Life of Dialogue.* (N.Y.: Harper and Brothers, 1960), Chapters III and IV.

41. Hodes, *op. cit.* p. 51.

42. Martin Buber, *Eclipse of God.* (N.Y.: Harper and Row, 1952), p. 7.

43. *Ibid.,* p. 8.

44. *Ibid.,* p. 9.

45. Martin Buber, *I and Thou,* Walter Kaufman, tr. (N.Y.: Charles Scribner's Sons, 1970), p. 127. Kaufman's in-

troduction is particularly helpful in placing Buber's work within a philosophical perspective.

46. F. R. Tennant, *Philosophical Theology*, Vol. II, *op. cit.*, p. 101. Tennant is very close to the position of W. R. Sorley, *Moral Values and the Idea of God.* (Cambridge: At the University Press, 1921). A more recent statement attempting to justify God's existence on the basis of an objective order of morality that can be apprehended by the natural intellect and that is ultimately grounded in the righteousness of God is a book by H. P. Owen, *The Moral Argument for Christian Theism.* (London: George Allen and Unwin Ltd., 1965).

47. Erich Fromm, *The Sane Society.* (N.Y.: Rinehart and Co., 1955), Chapter 3, pp. 22-66.

48. Fromm, *op. cit., Man for Himself,* pp. 145 ff.

49. Maslow's understanding of man's fundamental needs are: (1) Survival; (2) Security or safety; (3) Belongingness or love; (4) Esteem; (5) Growth or self-actualization. See his *Toward a Psychology of Being.* (Princeton: D. Van Nostrand Co., Inc., 1952) and his *The Farther Reaches of Human Nature.* (N.Y.: The Viking Press, 1971).

50. Walter A. Weisskopf, "Existence and Values," in Abraham Maslow, Ed. *New Knowledge in Human Values.* (N.Y.: Harper and Brothers, 1959), p. 109.

51. A. C. Garnett, *The Moral Nature of Man.* (N.Y.: The Ronald Press, 1952) p. 162.

52. *Kant: Selections.* Ed. by Theodore M. Greene, (N.Y.: Charles Scribner's Sons, 1957), p. 370, section entitled, "Modification of the Moral Proof of God's Existence in Kant's Opus Postumum," pp. 370 ff.

53. Immanuel Kant, *Foundations of the Metaphysics of Morals,* Tr. by Lewis White Beck. (Indianapolis: The Bobbs-Merrill Co., Inc., 1959), pp. 39 ff.

54. There are so many current books on Zen that it is difficult to mention only a few, but I think the following may not be as well known to the reader as some of the writings of the more widely read interpreters: Eugene Herrigel, *Zen in the Art of Archery*. (N.Y.: Vintage Books, 1953); Yoel Hoffmann, *The Sound of One Hand*. (N.Y.: Basic Books Inc., 1975); Ken Noyle, *Gone Tomorrow: Zen Inspired Poetry*. (Rutland, Vt.: Charles E. Tuttle, Co., 1966); Zenkei Shibayana, *Zen Comments on the Mumonkan*. (N.Y.: Harper and Row, 1974); Okakura Kakuzo, *The Book of Tea*. (Rutland, Vt.: Charles E. Tuttle, Co., 1956).
55. *The Republic*, Jowett tr. Book III, 401C.
56. Peter A. Bertocci, *Introduction to the Philosophy of Religion*. (N.Y.: Prentice-Hall, Inc., 1951) p. 380. Both Tennant and Bertocci have been suggestive for my development of this section of the chapter, particularly their emphasis upon the "cumulative argument for the existence of God."
57. John Elof Boodin, *God: A Cosmic Philosophy of Religion*. (N.Y.: The Macmillan Company, 1934), p. 117.
58. William Ernest Hocking, *The Coming World Civilization*. (N.Y.: Harper and Brothers, 1956). An excellent discussion of the interface between the great religions of mankind without jeopardizing the integrity of each.
59. Thomas Merton, "Monastic Experience and East-West Dialogue," in *The Asian Journal of Thomas Merton*. (London: Sheldon Press, 1974), pp. 309 ff.
60. C.A. Coulson, *Science and Christian Belief*. (London: Oxford University Press, 1955), p. 30.
61. Thomas Merton, *The Asian Journal*. Copyright 1973 by the Trustees of the Merton Legacy. Reprinted by permission of New Direction. Pp. 318, 319.